A Robbie Reader

What's So
Great About . . . ?
THE DONNER PARTY

Susan Sales Harkins and
William H. Harkins

P.O. Box 196
Hockessin, Delaware 19707
Visit us on the web: www.mitchelllane.com
Comments? email us: mitchelllane@mitchelllane.com

Printing   1   2   3   4   5   6   7   8   9

A Robbie Reader
What's So Great About . . . ?

Amelia Earhart	Anne Frank	Annie Oakley
Christopher Columbus	Daniel Boone	Davy Crockett
The Donner Party	Elizabeth Blackwell	Ferdinand Magellan
Francis Scott Key	Galileo	George Washington Carver
Harriet Tubman	Helen Keller	Henry Hudson
Jacques Cartier	Johnny Appleseed	King Tut
Lewis and Clark	Martin Luther King Jr.	Paul Bunyan
Pocahontas	Robert Fulton	Rosa Parks
Sam Houston		

Library of Congress Cataloging-in-Publication Data
Harkins, Susan Sales.
   The Donner Party / by Susan Sales Harkins and William H. Harkins.
      p. cm. — (A Robbie reader. What's so great about . . . ?)
   Includes bibliographical references and index.
   ISBN 978-1-58415-669-7 (library bound)
   1. Donner Party—Juvenile literature. 2. Pioneers—California—Biography—Juvenile literature. 3. Pioneers—California—Biography—Juvenile literature. 4. Pioneers—West (U.S.)—Biography—Juvenile literature. 5. Overland journeys to the Pacific—Juvenile literature. 6. Frontier and pioneer life—West (U.S.)—Juvenile literature. 7. Sierra Nevada (Calif. and Nev.)—History—19th century—Juvenile literature. I. Harkins, William H. II. Title.
   F868.N5H35 2009
   978'.02—dc22
                                                                                    2008020900

ABOUT THE AUTHORS: Susan and William Harkins live in Kentucky, where they enjoy writing together for children. Susan has written many books for adults and children. William is a history buff. In addition to writing, he is a member of the Air National Guard.

PUBLISHER'S NOTE: The following story has been thoroughly researched and to the best of our knowledge represents a true story. While every possible effort has been made to ensure accuracy, the publisher will not assume liability for damages caused by inaccuracies in the data, and makes no warranty on the accuracy of the information contained herein.

PLB

TABLE OF CONTENTS

Words in **bold** type can be found in the glossary.

George Donner, a successful farmer in Springfield, Illinois, eventually became the captain of the doomed Donner Party. We don't know if the photographs identified as George Donner are actually of him or of his nephew, George. When the Donners left Springfield, George was about 60 years old. He was tall with black eyes and black hair.

James Frazier Reed organized the group that left Springfield, Illinois, and eventually became known as the Donner Party. He was a successful businessman but thought he could do even better in California. His wife, Margaret, suffered from terrible headaches. They both hoped she would enjoy better health out west. They took their four children and Margaret's mother, Sarah Keyes. The elderly lady was sick and never made it to California. She died in Kansas.

"Chain Up, Boys!"

For months, the five Donner girls had listened to stories about California. There was plenty of land and the chance to make a fortune there. Then, on the morning of April 15, 1846, they peeped out the window and saw three covered wagons. They were going to California!

The first wagon contained seeds, tools, and other supplies they would need out west. Food, clothing, and camping tools filled the second wagon. In the last wagon, the girls would ride the 2,500 miles from Springfield, Illinois, to California.

"Chain up, boys! Chain up!" called George, their father.

That was the signal for the **teamsters** to get the wagons rolling. The girls climbed

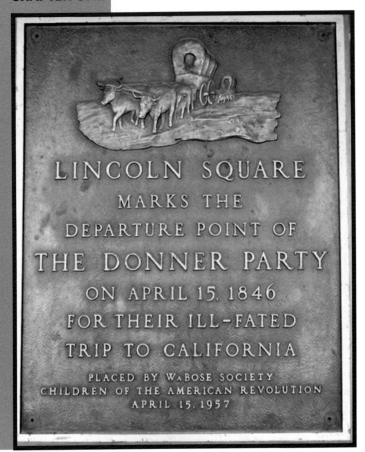

LINCOLN SQUARE
MARKS THE
DEPARTURE POINT OF
THE DONNER PARTY
ON APRIL 15, 1846
FOR THEIR ILL-FATED
TRIP TO CALIFORNIA
PLACED BY WABOSE SOCIETY
CHILDREN OF THE AMERICAN REVOLUTION
APRIL 15, 1957

In 1846, 1,500 people trekked across North America to California. A plaque in Lincoln Square in Springfield, Illinois, marks the beginning for a small group of pioneers, the Donners and the Reeds, that same year. Just three years later, 25,000 people made the trip when gold was found in California.

aboard. From the back of the last wagon, they watched their house, **orchard**, and cornfield disappear. The smallest child, Eliza, hugged her crying mother.

Some families had enough money to hire teamsters. These men drove the wagons and took care of the oxen. It was a helpful arrangement for everyone. The family had someone to drive their wagons, and the teamsters got a paid trip to California.

That night, the Donners camped just a few miles from home. Friends joined the **pioneers** for one last visit. Their campfire blazed high so that others back home could see. They sang songs, danced, and told stories. Late that night, their friends traveled home by moonlight.

The first day of their long journey was over. For the next five months, George and Tamsen Donner and their daughters planned to walk all day and camp each night until they reached San Francisco, California.

Members of the Donner and Reed wagon train celebrated Independence Day, 1846, at Fort Laramie. They made camp and had a huge dinner. A large party of Sioux Indians was at the fort. They exchanged gifts and made friends. When the wagon train left the fort, nearly three hundred Sioux warriors, riding in pairs, rode with them. Each warrior held a green twig or leaf in his mouth, a sign for peace.

A Fateful Decision

At first, the Donners traveled with a few other families from Springfield. Fathers led their wagons. Children ran through the tall **prairie** grass. They walked about two and a half miles an hour. On good days, they traveled ten to twelve miles.

In Kansas, they joined the Russell wagon train. The next morning, May 20, a loud trumpet blast woke them. By 7:00 A.M., they were on their way.

Curious Native Americans came to visit. The pioneers gave cloth, jewelry, tobacco, salt pork, and flour to them. In exchange for these items, the friendly Native Americans guarded the pioneers' cattle.

In late May, the pioneers left the gentle prairie. They used ropes and chains to guide the wagons up and down steep hills. It was a cold spring. Many people were sick. Near the Platte River, they started burning **buffalo chips** instead of wood in their campfires.

There was no doctor on the trail. Any injury was dangerous, but a bad injury could mean death. On June 14, a young boy died. Several days before, a wagon had rolled over his legs. A serious infection called gangrene set in. Another pioneer did his best to cut off the boy's legs to save his life. It was too late. The boy was too weak even to cry out in pain. He soon died. (A few pioneers wrote about the event in their diaries, but we don't know the child's name.) That same day, the pioneers celebrated a wedding, and a baby was born.

Most everyone planned to take the Oregon Trail to the west coast. George Donner had other plans. He had read *Emigrants' Guide to Oregon and California*. The author, Lansford W. Hastings, said there was a shorter route to California through the mountains called the Sierra Nevada. A friend from Illinois, James

Fort Bridger was a trading post built in 1843. James Bridger, a mountain man who discovered Bridger's Pass and Great Salt Lake, built it for trading furs and other items with Native Americans. It grew to include supplies for pioneers on the Oregon Trail.

Clyman, advised Donner not to take this trail, but Donner did not listen.

On July 19, the Russell wagon train reached a fork in the road. Most of the wagons took the path north toward Fort Hall (in present-day Idaho). The Donners, the Reeds, and a few other families took the path south to Fort Bridger (in present-day Wyoming)–toward Hastings Cutoff.

That night, the small wagon train chose George Donner as their leader. They called themselves the Donner Party. Their hopes were high. No one knew what horrors lay ahead.

Charles Stanton was a single businessman from Chicago. On or about September 12, 1846, he and William McCutchen rode ahead of the party. They planned to return with much-needed supplies from California. He could have stayed in California, but he kept his promise and came back with the supplies. In trying to help the pioneers, he sealed his own fate. Exhausted and starving, he froze to death in the mountains, alone.

William McCutchen was just 30 years old when he set out with Charles Stanton. Together, they crossed the mountains, blazing through unknown territory. By the time the two reached Fort Sutter, McCutchen was too sick for the return trip. Later, he joined the second relief group. He and his wife Amanda survived that winter, but their infant daughter, Harriet, died on or about February 2, 1847—just a few weeks before the first rescue party arrived.

Hastings Cutoff

In early August, the Donner Party left Fort Bridger. Their trail led southwest through Hastings Cutoff. There was no trail like there had been before. The men had to cut down trees to make a new trail. Most days, they traveled only a few miles, up and down steep **foothills**. Once, it took a full day to get all the wagons over just one hill!

The work was hard and the August sun was hot. It was about to get even hotter. On August 28, they reached a desert. They walked through **searing** heat during the day. At night, they wrapped themselves in blankets against the cold and walked some more. If they stopped to rest, the oxen, horses, and cattle might die of thirst.

The trip across the desert took longer than they had planned. Thirst drove the cattle crazy, and many ran into the desert. Almost every family lost cattle or oxen. The Reed family lost most of their cattle and had to leave two wagons behind. They had been the richest family in the group. When they came out of the desert, they were the poorest.

After losing most of their cattle, the group's food supplies ran low fast. The snow-covered mountains in the distance reminded everyone that winter was close. They must make it through the pass before the winter snow blocked it! Charles Stanton and William McCutchen rode ahead. They would bring supplies back from California.

Tired and hungry, people began to argue. During the day, the families traveled alone to avoid fighting. On October 6, they **banished** James Reed for killing John Snyder. Reed said he was protecting himself and his wife, Margaret. Many witnesses agreed with his story. Those who didn't agree wanted to hang

The sand in the Great Salt Desert contains so much salt that it is white. The Donner Party hiked 80 miles to get across it, which took several days. At night it was bitterly cold. Finally they reached a spring (now called Donner Spring) at the base of Pilot Peak. Once they were across, they spent several more days trying to gather the scattered cattle. The delay would cost them dearly.

Reed. In the end, they forced him to travel alone.

The Reeds thought the worst had happened to them—but their situation was about to get much more frightening.

View of Donner Lake, painted around 1872, is one of Albert Bierstadt's most famous paintings. During his trips west, Bierstadt made sketches. Back home in New York, he turned those sketches into huge landscapes. The Donner Party did not see the summit this way. All they saw was snow and ice.

Trapped!

The Donner Party lost a lot of cattle and horses in the desert. Then the Paiute Indians stole most of what was left (some say they did this after pioneers burned the food the Paiutes had stored for the winter). Everyone would starve if Charles Stanton and William McCutchen didn't return soon with food.

On October 23, they were overjoyed to meet Stanton on the trail. He led two Native American guides, named Luis and Salvadore, and several pack mules loaded with supplies. McCutchen had been too ill to make the return trip. The supplies refreshed the Donner Party, but there wasn't enough. The travelers were still weak and exhausted.

Two days later, the Breen family started up the last mountain. Other families followed slowly—all except George Donner's family. They were several miles behind. They had stopped to fix a broken axle.

On November 3, low clouds hid the pass. It was snowing hard already! Quickly, everyone except the Donners (who were still far behind) abandoned their wagons. Each adult grabbed a child, and they all ran for the **summit**. They had to get to the other side of the mountain quickly! Sadly, they were too weak from hunger for such hard work. They stumbled and fell in the deep snow.

They set a pine tree on fire and stopped to rest. Stanton shouted at them to get up, but they couldn't. The two Native American guides pointed to a ring around the moon. That meant more snow, they warned.

The Donner Party could go no farther. They fell asleep in the snow.

That night, more snow fell, blocking the pass. The Donner Party was trapped on the wrong side of the mountain with almost no food and no shelter.

The Donner Party made shelters using brush wrapped in blankets. They huddled together, trying to stay warm in the cold, wet, windy camp.

That winter, 37 adults and 44 children* camped on the east side of the summit. Every day they watched the mountain for rescuers.

*Sources vary on the exact number. Not all the pioneers were on the original manifest (list of travelers). At least six people died before reaching the winter camp.

As the pioneers grew colder and hungrier, some of them decided to leave camp and go for help. They made snowshoes and began their desperate journey over the pass.

A Ghastly Choice

The winter of 1846 was a nightmare for the Donner Party. Most lived near Truckee Lake, in shacks and lean-tos covered with buffalo **hides**. The Donners spent the winter in tents a few miles down the trail. A few families still had cattle. They charged high prices for the meat. Some men hunted wild birds and deer, but there was never enough to eat.

By December 1, the cattle were gone. Charles Stanton's pack mules were missing. The campers roasted mice and boiled hides for soup. Everyone suffered from **malnutrition**. Many people were sick.

A few adults made snowshoes out of twigs and hides. On December 16, they headed for the summit. The group, called the Forlorn

Hope, stumbled around for days, lost in the snow. One by one, they began to die. Starving and cold, they made a dreadful choice. They sliced the **flesh** from a dead body. Most of them cried as they ate their companion.

Finally, some Native Americans led a few of them to a white settlement in California. After hearing about the trapped pioneers, the Californians quickly put together a rescue team. They reached the Donner Party on February 19. They found nothing but white mounds of snow.

They called out, "Hello!"

A woman's head popped up through the snow. She said, "Are you men from California or are you from heaven?"

Starved campers crawled from their snow-covered cabins. They cried and laughed. The rescue party led several survivors over the mountain to safety. Many had to stay behind. The food the rescue party left behind ran out quickly. Rather than starve to death, they dug up dead bodies for food.

The Donner Party was not the only group of people to suffer hardship on their way west. From the 1840s to the 1860s, 10,000 pioneers died on the Oregon Trail. They died from wounds and disease. Over the Great Plains, desert, and then mountains, the pioneers walked, day after day. They ate biscuits, pancakes, dried beans, and fresh game. When the weather was bad, they continued to walk, through driving rain, thick mud, and searing heat.

Family	Parents	Dependent Children	Extended Family and Friends	Employees
Reed	James and Margaret	Virginia, Martha, James Jr., Thomas	Sarah Keyes	Hiram Miller, Walter Herron, Eliza Williams, Baylis Williams, James Smith, Milford Elliot
McCutchen	William and Amanda	Harriet		
Graves	Franklin and Elizabeth	Mary, William, Eleanor, Lovina, Nancy, Jonathan, Franklin Jr., Elizabeth	Sarah Graves Fosdick and Jay Fosdick	John Snyder
Murphy	Lavina	William, Landrum, Mary, Lemuel, Simon	Sarah Murphy Foster and William Foster: George Harriet Murphy Pike and William Pike: Naomi, Catherine	
Eddy	William and Eleanor	James, Margaret		
Donner	Jacob and Elizabeth	George, Mary, Isaac, Samuel, Lewis, Solomon Hook, William Hook		
Donner	George and Tamsen	Elitha, Leanna, Frances, Georgia, Eliza	Luke Halloran, John Denton, Charles Stanton	John Baptiste Trudeau, Noah James, Samuel Shoemaker, Antonio (full name unknown)
Keseberg	Lewis and Philippine	Ada, Lewis Jr.	Mr. Hardkoop (full name unknown)	Charles Berger (teamster; some historians place him with the Donner family)
Wolfinger	Mr. [first name not certain] and Doris			
Breen	Patrick and Margaret	John, Edward, Patrick Jr., Simon, James, Peter, Isabella	Patrick Dolan	
OTHERS	Joseph Reinhardt, Augustus Spitzer, Salvadore, Luis			

Many families and several individuals were part of the Donner Party. This chart shows who lived and who died (the names of those who died are in *italic type*). A 🪣 shows who died before reaching the mountains. A ⚫ shows who was a member of Forlorn Hope. Salvadore and Luis were the Native American guides who returned with Charles Stanton; they were murdered for food by William Foster.

Over the next few months, three more rescue parties arrived. Each time, they took a few more survivors over the mountain.

That winter, 37 members of the Donner Party died. Except for the elderly Sarah Keyes (who died in Kansas), no one in the Reed or Breen families died. Only the Reed family refused to eat human flesh to survive.

Neither George nor Tamsen Donner made it to California. When rescuers arrived, George was too sick to travel. A wound was infected and he was slowly dying. Tamsen, who refused

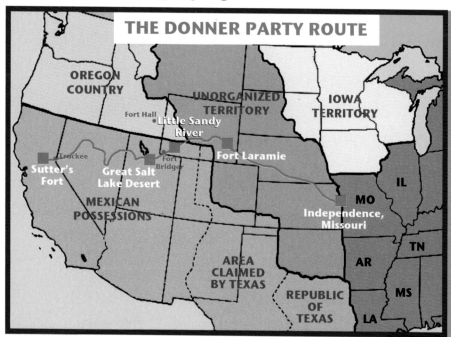

THE DONNER PARTY ROUTE

OREGON COUNTRY

UNORGANIZED TERRITORY

IOWA TERRITORY

Fort Hall

Little Sandy River

Truckee

Fort Bridger

Fort Laramie

Sutter's Fort

Great Salt Lake Desert

IL

MEXICAN POSSESSIONS

MO

Independence, Missouri

TN

AREA CLAIMED BY TEXAS

AR

REPUBLIC OF TEXAS

MS

LA

The Donner Party set out from Independence, Missouri, on May 11, 1846. Nearly a year later—on April 25, 1847—the last survivor reached Sutter's Fort in California.

Many believe this antique wagon on a ranch in Nevada belonged to the Donner Party. We don't know for sure if this wagon was part of the Donner wagon train, but it is similar to the wagons they used. It took four to eight oxen to pull each wagon across the plains and over the mountains.

to leave her sick husband to die alone, sent her girls over the summit with the rescue party.

Tamsen's death is a mystery. Lewis Keseberg told rescuers that she fell asleep and died the day after George died. Rescuers never found her body.

Reporters wrote about the trapped Donner Party. Many of their stories were lies. Some accused them all of murdering their weaker companions for food. The truth is, during a desperate time, the members of the Donner Party did what they had to do to survive.

CHRONOLOGY

1846

April 15	The Reed and Donner families leave Springfield, Illinois.
May 11	They arrive at Independence, Missouri.
May 29	Sarah Keyes, who is over 70 years old, dies in Kansas Territory.
July 20	The Donner Party splits from the Russell party and heads south for Fort Bridger. George Donner is named leader.
July 26–30	The Donner Party rests at Fort Bridger.
July 31	They leave Fort Bridger for Hastings Cutoff.
August	They cut a wagon trail through the Wasatch Mountains (Utah).
August 25	Luke Halloran dies.
Early September	The Donner Party crosses the Great Salt Desert (Utah).
September 10	Charles Stanton and William McCutchen ride ahead to bring back supplies.
October 5	James Reed is banished after killing teamster John Snyder.
October 8	Mr. Hardkoop is abandoned to die along the trail.
October 13	Mr. Wolfinger dies. Reinhardt and Spitzer are suspected of foul play, but they blame his death on an Indian attack.
October 21	William Pike dies of an accidental gunshot wound from his brother-in-law, William Foster.
October 25	Charles Stanton returns with supplies and two Native American guides (Luis and Salvadore).
November 3	The Donner Party attempts to climb to the summit before snow falls; they fail.
November 4	The party makes camp at the base of the mountain, near Truckee Lake.
December 16	Forlorn Hope, a group of 15, leaves the camp for California.
December 25	Members of Forlorn Hope are the first to eat the flesh of a fallen companion.

CHRONOLOGY

1847

January 10	William Foster murders Luis and Salvadore, the Native American guides, for food.
Mid-January	Native Americans lead Forlorn Hope survivors to white settlement in California.
January 31	First rescue group sets out.
February 19	First rescue group reaches the survivors; 22 members of the Donner Party travel to California with their help.
February 27	The Reeds are reunited when James Reed finds his wife and two of his children on the trail with the first relief party. James Reed travels on to the lake camp to rescue his other two children.
March 1	Second rescue team reaches survivors. They are horrified to find mutilated bodies at the lake shelters. Some had resorted to cannibalism to survive.
March 5	James Reed leads 17 survivors across the summit and into California, where they are trapped by a snowstorm. After a few days, they move on, but the Breens and a few others stay behind to wait for the next relief party. They huddle together as a small fire melts the snow. They sink 15 feet before reaching bare ground. They call their pit Starved Camp.
March 12	Members of Starved Camp begin eating the dead.
March 13	Third rescue team reaches Starved Camp and the lake survivors; all but five of the survivors start for California.
March 27	George Donner dies; his wife, Tamsen, dies the next day.
April 18	Fourth rescue team reaches lone survivor, Lewis Keseberg.
April 25	Lewis Keseberg, the last survivor, reaches safety in California.
June 22	The lake camp is burned by U.S. Army soldiers.

TIMELINE IN HISTORY

1803   Lewis and Clark set out from St. Louis, Missouri, for the Pacific Ocean on their journey of discovery across the North American continent.

1814   The British burn Washington, D.C., in the War of 1812.

1832   Joe Walker and Benjamin Bonneville blaze a trail across the Rocky Mountains to California.

1836   Texas freedom fighters fall to Mexican forces at the Battle of the Alamo.

1843   Jim Bridger, who had discovered Great Salt Lake, builds Fort Bridger in what will be Wyoming. The first great wave of settlers arrive in Oregon by the Oregon Trail.

1845   John Chapman (Johnny Appleseed) dies after spending almost 50 years planting apple trees from Pennsylvania to Indiana. Texas becomes a state.

1848   Gold is discovered in California, sparking the California Gold Rush.

1850   California becomes a state.

1861   The Confederates fire against Fort Sumter, and the Civil War begins.

1869   The railroad is completed across the United States.

FIND OUT MORE

Books

Calabro, Marian. *The Perilous Journey of the Donner Party*. New York: Clarion Books, 1999.*

Laurgaard, Rachel K. *Patty Reed's Doll: The Story of the Donner Party*. Davis, California: Tomato Enterprises, 1989.*

Lavender, David. *Snowbound: The Tragic Story of the Donner Party*. New York: Holiday House, 1996.*

Mercati, Cynthia. *Longest Journey: The Story of the Donner Party*. Logan, Iowa: Perfection Learning, 2002.

Wachtel, Roger. *The Donner Party*. New York: Children's Press, 2003.

Welvaert, Scott R. *The Donner Party*. Mankato, Minnesota: Capstone Press, 2006.

*These older editions remain recommended reading in many schools and contain relevant information for today's youth.

FIND OUT MORE

Works Consulted

Hardesty, Donald L. *The Archaeology of the Donner Party*. Reno: University of Nevada Press, 1997.

Johnson, Kristin (editor). *Unfortunate Emigrants: Narratives of the Donner Party*. Logan: Utah State University Press, 1996.

Keithley, George. *The Donner Party*. New York: George Braziller, Inc., 1989.

King, Joseph A. *Winter of Entrapment*. Toronto: P. D. Meany Publishers, 1992.

McGlashan, C. F. *History of the Donner Party*. Stanford, California: Stanford University Press, 1947.

Mullen, Frank, Jr. *The Donner Party Chronicles*. Reno: Nevada Humanities Committee, 1997.

Pigney, Joseph. *For Fear We Shall Perish*. New York: E. P. Dutton & Co., Inc., 1961.

Stewart, George R. *Ordeal by Hunger*. London: Ere & Spottiswoode, Ltd., 1960.

On the Internet

American Experience: The Donner Party: The Breen Diary
    http://www.pbs.org/wgbh/amex/donner/sfeature/sf_diary.html
California State Parks: Donner Memorial State Park
    http://www.parks.ca.gov/?page_id=503
Donner Online
    http://www.kn.pacbell.com/wired/donner/index.html
Donner Party Family Camp Archaeology Project
    http://www.anthro.umt.edu/donner/history.htm
Forensics of the Donner Party
    http://raiboy.tripod.com/Donner/id14.html
The Hastings Trail
    http://www.xmission.com/~octa/RTFrames.htm
New Light on the Donner Party
    http://www.xmission.com/~octa/DonnerParty/
Survivors of the Donner Party
    http://members.aol.com/DanMRosen/donner/survivor.htm
We're Hitting the Trail: The Donner Party
    http://www.donnerpartydiary.com/

GLOSSARY

banish (BAA-nish)—To kick someone out of a group.

buffalo chip (BUH-fuh-loh CHIP)—A piece of dried buffalo dung.

destiny (DES-tuh-nee)—Something that is supposed to happen.

flesh (FLESH)—An animal's skin, fat, and muscles.

foothill (FOOT-hil)—A hill at the base of a mountain.

hide (hyd)—An animal's skin.

malnutrition (mal-noo-TRIH-shun)—Unhealthy condition when the body doesn't get a balanced diet.

orchard (OR-cherd)—A group of trees, usually fruit or nut trees.

pioneer (pye-uh-NEER)—Someone who is among the first to travel through or settle a new region.

prairie (PRAY-ree)—A large area of flat grassland with few trees.

searing (SEER-ing)—Burning.

summit (SUH-mit)—The top of a mountain.

teamster (TEEM-ster)—A person who drives a team of horses or cattle.

PHOTO CREDITS: Cover, pp. 6, 15, 26—Barbara Marvis; pp. 1, 3—Historic Donner Trail.org; p. 4 (bottom)—AP/Utah State Historical Society; pp. 4 (top), 12—Eliza P. Donner Houghton; p. 8—Alfred Jacob Miller; p. 11—W. H. Jackson; p. 16—Albert Bierstadt; pp. 19, 20, 23—North Wind Picture Archives; pp. 24, 25—Sharon Beck.

INDEX

14(0)

25 99

"This book is a must-read for church leaders who want to build life-transforming small groups that can reach the lost and radically change this generation."

—PETE WILSON, senior pastor, Cross Point Church, Nashville; author of *Plan B* and *Empty Promises*

"Imagine someone dumping ten gallons of ice water on your head. That's how I felt reading the first chapters of this book. Rick exposes our broken and post-Christian society (and our failed attempts to reach it) with shocking clarity. Then he offers a Christ-centered, relational, and biblical warm towel in the form of an in-depth explanation of Christian micro-communities and their potential impact on our society if we'll just do church differently. What an excellent, practical, and motivational read!"

—RANDALL NEIGHBOUR, president, TOUCH Outreach Ministries; author of *The Naked Truth About Small Group Ministry*

"Rick Howerton has been a consistent voice of encouragement and guidance in both my personal discipleship and the strategic decisions I make to mobilize the communities of transformation that I lead. I'm grateful that his unique voice is now only an arm's length away on my shelf as he invites us to abandon programs in favor of relationships. *A Different Kind of Tribe* is not simply a handbook; it is an invitation to play a role in the greatest challenge ever given: to make disciples."

—HEATHER ZEMPEL, discipleship pastor, National Community Church, Washington, DC; author of *Wineskins for Discipleship*

"It's about time Rick shared his rich experience and wisdom about groups! But he's given us more than that. He's called us to renew a timeless value: communal life in the church. This book is a keeper, and I recommend that you read it carefully if you plan on being neck deep in building biblical community through small groups."

—BILL DONAHUE, PhD, best-selling author of
Leading Life-Changing Small Groups

"Rick Howerton continues to challenge and shape our thinking when it comes to what small groups look like in our ever-changing world."

—MARGARET FEINBERG, speaker; idea wrestler;
author of *The Organic God*

"Rick weaves a beautifully accurate picture of 'idyllic' America that has been dismantled by postmodern society. And instead of simply railing against it, he gives a compelling, biblical, Christ-exalting, and community-centered call to action for the church. I've been leading small groups and training small-group leaders for years. Rick has put words to what I have found to be the successful aspects of group life. This will prove to be an indispensable resource for group leaders."

—BEN REED, small-groups pastor,
Grace Community Church, Clarksville, Tennessee;
marketing and communications director, The Small Group Network

A DIFFERENT KIND OF
TRIBE

EMBRACING THE NEW SMALL-GROUP DYNAMIC

RICK HOWERTON

NavPress

Discipleship Inside Out®

Discipleship Inside Out®

NavPress is the publishing ministry of The Navigators, an international Christian organization and leader in personal spiritual development. NavPress is committed to helping people grow spiritually and enjoy lives of meaning and hope through personal and group resources that are biblically rooted, culturally relevant, and highly practical.

For a free catalog go to www.NavPress.com

NavPress titles may be purchased in bulk for ministry, educational, business, fund-raising, or sales promotional use. For information, please call NavPress Special Markets at 1.800.504.2924.

ISBN-13: 978-1-61747-995-3
ISBN-13: 978-1-61291-347-6 (electronic)

Cover design by Arvid Wallen
Cover illustration by Shutterstock/earthvector

Some of the anecdotal illustrations in this book are true to life and are included with the permission of the persons involved. All other illustrations are composites of real situations, and any resemblance to people living or dead is coincidental.

Unless otherwise identified, all Scripture quotations in this publication are taken from *The Holy Bible, English Standard Version* (ESV), copyright © 2001 by Crossway Bibles, a division of Good News Publishers. Used by permission. All rights reserved. Other versions used include: the *Holy Bible, New International Version*® (NIV®). Copyright © 1973, 1978, 1984 by Biblica, used by permission of Zondervan. All rights reserved; and *THE MESSAGE* (MSG). Copyright © 1993, 1994, 1995, 1996, 2000, 2001, 2002. Used by permission of NavPress Publishing Group.

Howerton, Rick.
    A different kind of tribe : embracing the new small-group dynamic / Rick Howerton.
        p. cm.
    Includes bibliographical references (p.   ).
    ISBN 978-1-61747-995-3
    1. Church group work. 2. Small groups. I. Title.
    BV652.2.H69 2012
    253'.7—dc23
                                                2012000216

Printed in the United States of America

1 2 3 4 5 6 7 8 / 17 16 15 14 13 12

*This book is dedicated to Dan Flanagan, Tom Smoot, and
Mel Doughty—three mentors, brothers, and friends
who not only modeled and taught me to think
outside the box but also encouraged me in it.*

CONTENTS

INTRODUCTION

God did not randomly drop any of us onto planet Earth. With unfathomable discernment He positioned each of us with very personal curiosities and passions in a given era. My inescapable obsessions are interviewing, researching, reading, training, networking, mentoring, responding to questions about and partnering with other persons passionate about small groups, and being a small-group leader and coach at my own church. My years as a small-group pastor led me to believe this one fact: If there were a biblical small group within walking distance of every person on the planet, the world would see the gospel at work and hear it from the lips of those who are living it.

I've been honored that small-group aficionados in the most influential roles and some serving the most influential churches have been open to a relationship with me. I am in waters way above my head and remind myself daily that drowning in these waters would be a great honor.

We are inundated with information about small groups and ways to do groups. It seems every influential church has built a model of its own, published a book, and is espousing it as either "the way to do small groups" or "the new way to do groups." I have read as many of these books as I possibly can and believe almost every one of them is important and has something substantial to say. But are we seeing so many ways to do group because many, many great church leaders know something is out of sync and are courageous enough to go looking for the answer?

A few years ago I began to ask myself: "Are the principles and practices being promoted again and again simply a rehashing of ideologies from a past era, an era that has come and gone?"

This book was written in response to my journey into this question. Here's the deal: I believe that the small-group movement cannot continue on its current trajectory or it will become just another neutered experience for already overprogrammed church types, church members whose greatest adventure is attending the next church-sponsored class, whose greatest sacrifice is dropping a few bucks into the offering plate as it goes by, individuals who will exit the local church as soon as it no longer makes them happy or is unable to shield them from the sinful, dark world that exists outside the four walls of the church building. The world has changed, the way we do group has not—but it must.

The wave of post-Christianity has come ashore. We must be willing to submerge ourselves in it as we did the first wave, modernity. We cannot escape this wave. It has come ashore without our requesting it or giving it permission to do so. The tsunami is upon us. We must experience life in the warmth of its seemingly untrustworthy waters.

We intuitively sense some of the wave's characteristics, especially when compared to other eras. But to paint a vivid picture of this new cultural force is impossible as its colors and borders are not well defined. Even an image that might depict its beauty is as unattainable as an artist attempting to paint the likeness of a future spouse, having never seen her before. The paradigm shift continues to resist being put in a box. We can recognize a few of its basic tenets—moral nothingness, self-governing individualism, narcissistic hedonism, and tolerance as a religion—but if the truth were known, this cultural change is revisited and revised constantly.

Know this: We live in and minister the post-Christian world, and that is the context in which we invite people to do life together in—in small groups. The mindset and culture we have been living in is no more, and I am certain that we, the small-group leaders or pastors, must recognize this and make adjustments as necessary.

Admit this: Each of us, at some level, is being affected by our existence in a post-Christian world. We exist in a post-Christian era and culture and it is influencing the way we view family, community, and life.

Accept this: Individuals involved in the group-life movement realize that the world has changed its view on many issues. Humankind's view of Christianity, morality, and the Bible has changed. The definitions of family, spirituality, and truth have changed. How we communicate, what we communicate, and why we communicate with one another have changed. Who influences us and the actions that allow us to trust those who lead us have changed.

It is my prayer that what you find in these pages will help all of us understand past realities, present realities, and how to see life transformation in an era not yet fully understood, with a people who are not yet fully aware that their own journey and the journey of their own small group have new paths to follow.

What you are about to read is not a new way to do groups, although I will be making some suggestions. You are about to take a journey into a paradigm, a paradigm that might cause you to rethink your group system or aid you in realizing you're way ahead of the game.

As you read, you'll want to keep a few things in mind:

1. This book is written for small-group leaders and pastors whose paradigm of a group includes those far from Christ coming from the many ideological perspectives and belief systems that are prevalent in this era, not just already-churched evangelical church members.
2. The letters CMC stand for Christian micro-community. I am hoping this phrase will impress upon each of us that a small group is not another program of the church—it is a small community of Christ followers being the church and pre-Christians watching them do that.
3. I love the church, work in and through churches, and have given my life to her. As you read this book, you'll see that I make some indictments concerning the church and some aspects of denominational life. I do not make these statements to degrade or dishonor either the local church or any denomination. I am simply pointing out facts that must be taken into consideration if we are going to see life transformation through CMCs in a post-Christian era.

RICK HOWERTON

CHAPTER 1

FACING A NEW REALITY

LIFE IN A ROCKWELLIAN WORLD

For nearly three decades, the Norman Rockwell print "Saying Grace" took up residence on one wall or another in every office I worked in. You may know the image. Let me see if I can describe it: It is the picture of a grandmother with three boys before a meal.[1] Grandma has her head bowed and is praying. The two teenage boys are mischievously checking out what's going on around the room. One thing is for sure—the boys realize their frank gaze is inappropriate and an act of rebellion and that Grandma is right in what she is doing. Grandma is following a societal norm, and these two young men are blatantly ignoring the norm.

Here's the reality: We once lived in a Rockwellian world. The West was once fully embedded in Judeo-Christian values and beliefs. The Americana depicted by this one image is a reminder of what once was: God was considered holy and worthy of reverence; public acts in response to His holiness (if not too outlandish) were seen by others as honorable and those involved in those practices were worthy of respect; and each generation was admired for embracing Christian beliefs and practices and was expected to pass those nonnegotiables on to the generations that followed. And those who painted outside the lines of this mindset were perceived as abnormal and out of sync with the rest of society.

But as a young girl who was transported by a tornado from her Rockwellian world to a whole new culture once put it, "We're not in Kansas anymore." The world has changed. In fact, a few more remembrances:

There used to be an understood order to life, including respecting those in leadership. I will not soon forget my first real job. I was a fifteen-year-old busboy at a 76 truck stop. The place was open twenty-four hours a day. My first run was the grave-yard shift. (Ya oughta know it's gonna be bad when you're workin' somethin' called the "graveyard shift.") There was a dog racetrack just a few miles from the place. (In case you're wondering, it's like Churchill Downs, only they race dogs instead of horses.) As soon as the races ended, about midnight, that restaurant filled up with customers and people were waiting in line.

One night I found myself overwhelmed. The place was so busy that I couldn't keep the tables cleaned fast enough, which meant the waitresses weren't going to get the amount of tips they deserved and I knew I was the problem. I was going as fast as I could, but there was no way I could clean the tables, scrape the plates, wipe off each table, and get the dishes back to the dishwasher quickly enough. There were angry eyes shooting daggers at me much of the night—waitress eyes. As you might imagine, after we got the dog-racing crowd out, that restaurant came to a standstill. I was left to face the two waitresses whose income I'd affected greatly. In the moment and in an effort to protect myself, I attacked the absent manager. I blurted out, "The boss oughta hire at least one more busboy! He can't expect one person to be able to get this work done! Doesn't he get it? If he doesn't do something about this, I'm just gonna quit." One of the waitresses called me to the side of the room. She then whispered, "Rick, if you're going to make it in this world, there's one thing you gotta get right. The guy in charge is always to be respected. Don't ever say anything to your boss that's disrespectful. That's just life."

I don't believe this woman was a follower of Christ. If she was, then one of her spiritual gifts was customer flirtation. She was simply schooling me on life in the era we were living in. Leaders were to be respected because they were the leaders, not because they'd earned someone's respect. They were to be respected because the title of "leader" had been bestowed on them.

And in the Norman Rockwell world, the leaders of leaders, the persons who should be respected most, were parents. Parents presided over the home and anyplace else where they were with their kids. In the Norman Rockwell society, a child seldom questioned a parent's decision or requests. "Honor your father and your mother" (Exodus 20:12) was more than just a cliché held to in a bygone era. It was one of the ten societal expectations that were ingrained in Western society.

But parents were, for the most part, worthy of respect. Why?

Being noble and honest was honored and a goal to attain in everyday situations and dealings. Living a life of integrity was more than an ideal for the old-fashioned nerd of nerds. It was anticipated that every decent person would keep any commitment he had made (whether that was keeping marriage vows or showing up to play a game of softball), hold his tongue when off-color or profane words came to mind, and never cheat (whether that be on a high school math test or on one's taxes). No one would be considered respectable if he or she chose to ignore the values of the time. These were societal norms and expectations that defined who received honor and who didn't.

The point: Because the social norms were in line with Judeo-Christian values, moral anarchy did not exist. Don't get me wrong; there was sin and it was rampant. Until Christ returns, this will just be a fact. But actions and activities that contradicted those values were considered unacceptable and out of sync with the value system of the time. Not so today.

WE'RE NOT IN KANSAS ANYMORE AND THERE'S NO YELLOW BRICK ROAD

One of the key reasons the Rockwellian era was so in line with Christian values is because, for the most part, the Western world considered the Bible the guide for living individual life and living in community. But the post-Christian era brought with it a cynicism about most things and most certainly cynicism concerning the Bible as foundational ideology. In the minds of the masses, the Bible transitioned from being considered words given us by the Creator of the universe, the God of Christianity, to an antique collection of sayings and stories unable to speak to the life and times of people in a new age.

For many wading the waters of a new era, the Bible was to be questioned solely because it seemed to have lost its relevancy. To others, morality without boundaries was the issue. After the sexual revolution of the sixties, society saw a slide into moral chaos. The Bible's demands were too confining. Not only did people want to "do their own thing," they wanted to do whatever was "right in their own eyes" (see Judges 17:6) without pulpiteers or followers of Christ questioning their choices. Shutting up or shutting out the voices that might remind someone of the inappropriateness of those choices was now necessary. This is how someone could rationalize living life contradictory to what had been required by God's law and what had been embraced by a prior generation.

In 1977, I made my way to study at a university. This was a new world for me. I now realize that shadows of the era to come were already beginning to throw shades of gray over society. I had been brought up in a pastor's home and was, for the first time, going to see the rest of the ideological world. The contrast between what was acceptable thinking back at the house and in the churches Dad served and what was acceptable thinking in some college classrooms and on the college campus was as different as the climate in Alaska in January and the climate on the sun.

God became a concept to be questioned, not a loving Father who created the universe and welcomed me into it. Sex was an exploratory expression of a couple out on a date, not something to wait until marriage to experience with someone to whom you had made a lifelong commitment. Social drinking no longer meant having a couple of drinks with a few friends; the social way to drink was to throw down as many as you possibly could at an out-of-control party while the rest of the room sang, "Here's to Rick, to Rick, to Rick. Here's to Rick, who's with us tonight. So drink chug-a-lugga, drink chug-a-lugga, drink chug-a-lugga, drink chug-a-lugga. Here's to Rick, who's with us tonight." And the Bible was the straight man for joke after joke, and those who embraced it in faith were considered fantasizers welcoming myths and antiquated expectations of a God who didn't exist.

Many bought into this mindset wholeheartedly, but for those who remembered the Rockwellian world, the still small voices of conviction or guilt that accompanied their acts of rebellion were louder than ever. College brought with it a new view of faith and the Bible and a lifestyle that kept the consciences of many hard at work. In time, they learned to shut the voices out, and the guilt subsided some.

But for many, the guilt didn't diminish by simply shutting out the voices and setting aside God's words. Whether it was due to the fact that the society they had been brought up in had invaded their hearts too deeply or because their parents continued to remind them or because the Holy Spirit was convicting them, they couldn't silence their own conscience. Shutting out the voices didn't get it done, so those running from the values of the past instinctively drowned them out. Because they wouldn't embrace God's truth, they created their own.

Many years later while on a flight from Atlanta to Nashville, I couldn't help but notice that one of the articles in the airline's magazine was titled "Speaking Her Truth." I had to read this one. The article focused on a celebrity, Melissa Etheridge. As I read down a few paragraphs, I found these words: "That strong self-direction has given rise to a constant description of Etheridge as 'authentic.' It makes her laugh. Etheridge is quoted as saying, 'Because of what people project on me—"She's so authentic," "She's speaking her truth"—all of a sudden, the greatest weapon I have is to seek it and speak it. I'm drunk with power! Every time I speak my truth, I am looked upon as being "courageous."'" I believe Etheridge described what many are embracing. When an individual courageously speaks his or her truth—even when it contradicts the only real truth, God's truth—and others embrace it, a generous empowerment takes place.

Bottom line: God's truth was too confining for a people ignoring His directives, so individuals created their own truth. And when "my truth" is truth, I can do whatever I choose without feeling guilt, considering the ways my decisions affect others, or being concerned with God's view of my actions. And, just like this celebrity, many fed off of the power that accompanies the belief that one's personal truth is the better truth.

Isn't this the ultimate form of idolatry? At this point, one has replaced God as the sole authority and made oneself the authority on all issues.

What did society lose when individual idolatry did an end run on God's authority? Healthy, biblical sexuality was traded in for no-holds-barred promiscuity. Seasonal, communal celebrations based on the church calendar were replaced by baseball, football, and basketball seasons. Marriage being between a man and a woman committed for life was replaced with an easy exit strategy anytime either party is no longer "happy." The primary focus of a parent's life being to raise God-honoring children (or at least good citizens) was replaced with surviving the parenting process. Children respecting parents and allowing parents to govern their lives was replaced with MTV-style questioning of parental authority and ignoring it when it contradicts with what their peers think is acceptable and normal.

With the extinction of a set of common values, accountability exited the culture. After all, how can someone question another person's choices if the choices are driven by each person's values, a truth of his or her own making?

Secularism not only invaded Western culture, it infiltrated almost every inch of the culture and has set up its own way. How did these new realities overtake cultural norms that were so deeply ingrained in the hearts of the masses?

CHAPTER 2

A DELICATE NOSEDIVE INTO THE NEW REALITY

When worlds abruptly collide, it's easy to note that something has gone horribly wrong. When transformation is slow, people may simply wake up one day and realize that all has changed. Our society seems to have done a delicate nosedive into the new reality that has overtaken us. This newness sneaked up on us because it invaded through our hearts, not by the establishment of new laws or official declarations demanding society think and live differently. The Enemy attacked us at the most vulnerable of all places, a place that would most deeply affect our thoughts and lifestyles—our hearts. And he did so by perverting those intimate relationships and ideals that make us who we are—our homes, our sexuality, our God, and through trusted leaders.

BROKEN SPHERES OF INFLUENCE

One of the Enemy's most brutal forms of attack is through **busted spheres or orbs of influence**. Every human who ever existed on planet Earth was created to be influenced by influencers. Some influencers influence more profoundly than others simply because of their God-given roles. But when these orbs of influence are broken, an individual is deeply affected.

Extended family is one of those busted orbs. We were made with an instinct to learn how to live life by watching the lives of extended family. We were meant to learn wisdom from family members who had lived long lives seeking God's wisdom. In ancient Israel, "Elders in a family were revered for their wisdom; and in everyday settings, they assumed responsibilities for transferring their knowledge and insights to the young."[1]

Living among extended family can be either positive or negative, for sure. In a spiritually and emotionally healthy family system, much can be gained in the establishment of right thinking and spiritual nurture. Grandparents, uncles and aunts, and other relatives are models and/or mentors for the next generation. With models of biblical living and spiritual health, the next generation of believers has a much firmer foundation on which to stand. When someone has to move away, the extended family's influence in terms of lifestyle, ideals, and spiritual practices greatly diminishes. Those on the move may land in a place void of extended family. And it would be very unusual for anyone to influence someone as deeply as a spiritually mature grandparent could. Let's face it—when a spiritually healthy extended family is within arm's reach, the influence is beyond comprehension.

I know this firsthand. My older brother and his wife established their home in Franklin, Tennessee. It had always been their goal to have my parents live with them. When purchasing his home, my brother chose a house that let my parents have a downstairs apartment. A few years after my parents moved in, I took a job in the same city and moved within three miles of where my brother's family and my parents lived. My brother is the father of two incredible adult children. Both of them are abnormal in their generation when it comes to being driven to Scripture. Both of them are abnormal in their generation when it comes to boldness in speaking of Christ. Both of them are abnormal in their generation as they have strong opinions and great grace when it comes to morality and right living. Both of them exhibit characteristics that are true of their parents, their aunt and uncle, and their grandparents. I have no doubt that being brought up near extended family who modeled and reinforced what parents were already teaching helped make them the people they are today.

Don't get me wrong. I'm not suggesting that families should stay put. I'm simply pointing out one of the changes that has affected our hearts and created the new reality we live in today.

Another orb that has become less and less a part of the new reality is **long-term friendships**. According to some experts, the average U.S. resident will move a total of sixteen times over his or her lifetime, about once every five years. Not many people spend face-to-face time consistently with someone they've known for even a decade. Deep friendships have become a short-term expression at best. Because this is true, few people in our sphere of face-to-face relationships know our full story. They know only the fragment of story we unveil.

Our "new friends," the friends we will connect with only until the next move, may never know that our father was an abusive alcoholic. They may never know that you as an adult fear the dark because someone once broke into your home in the night and attacked your family. They may never know that you left "the church" because a pastor you once respected had an affair or was spiritually abusive to the congregation, causing you to lose trust in all pastors. They may never know that you are hesitant to dive into a dating relationship that could lead to marriage because your last spouse bailed on you for no apparent reason. They may never know that you dream of getting a college degree, starting your own business, or becoming a college professor.

When long-term friendships became a thing of the past, a new relational reality was established, a reality that lets someone remain in a land of half-truths and wholehearted denial. Putting on false fronts became much easier, hiding behind the facade created in each new setting became possible, and never being called upon to wrestle with the parts of your story that hold you captive became the new norm. We exist in short-term friendships to feel connected, but we are seldom known well enough to be called upon to confront our inner demons or to be reminded of and encouraged to accomplish our greatest dreams.

With these two relational orbs in disarray, we lost an aspect of the Christian life that is a foundation for healthy spirituality—**spiritual memories**. Spiritual memories are mental snapshots of those we love and respect acting out spiritual practices. Spiritual memories are memories that are ingrained deeply in our hearts. Seeing a grandparent praying at the church's altar, an uncle reading Scripture before the Thanksgiving meal, the adult baptism of a friend someone has known since grammar school, the laying on of hands and praying over a sin-wrestling peer we've known since high school, all are illustrations of spiritual memories that invade our hearts and inspire us to live our lives in ways that bring glory to God. When a life is void of these memories, it lacks moments that establish God and His people as real and vital to a person's life. They also instill intuitive responses to life situations that believers find themselves in.

These two shattered orbs—extended family and long-term friendships—are deeply affecting the hearts of those who are attending your Christian micro-communities. The beauty of Christian micro-communities is that they are the best response to these busted orbs. In the chapters that follow, you'll find out that God has always planned for the body of Christ to be the life-giving response to the societal changes we are experiencing. But for now, let's establish that these two aspects of the human experience aided in the nosedive into the new reality in which we all exist.

But it's not only these two orbs that promoted the plunge. More choices, influencers, and perversions contributed to our landing in the new reality.

FAMILY DYSFUNCTION

Our culture has amnesia when it comes to two marriage partners becoming one for a lifetime. We have forgotten what it means to marry for life and instead have embraced a "you better make me happy or I'm outta here" mentality. With little or no consideration for the effects of divorce on children, couples are walking out on one another ad nauseum. According to research by Jennifer Baker, director of the marriage- and family-therapy programs at Forest Institute, a postgraduate psychology school in Springfield, Missouri, 50 percent of first marriages, 67 percent of second, and 74 percent of third marriages end in divorce.[2]

Very few experiences affect someone's relationship to the Christian community as deeply as when parents divorce or family dysfunction is present. The authors of *Lost and Found: The Younger Unchurched and the Churches That Reach Them* researched the effects of divorce on young adults and how it affects their relationship with the church and small groups. They found:

> Divorce rates are high and single-parent homes are becoming more the norm. Parental presence has been absent in many young people's lives. This is not always a result of marital strife or even

death within the family unit. In many cases young adults were simply ignored or mistreated by their parents. These circumstances do impact the context in which individuals approach community.[3]

Some ideas root deeply into the heart of young people whose parents split, and these ideas may affect the way these individuals function in relation to the CMC they are part of.

Rick and Kathy Roepke are friends of mine who own the Christian Family Institute in Bowling Green, Kentucky. These counselors with decades of experience tell us that divorce affects three aspects of the heart and ultimately how people function in a CMC:

Trust seems to be a major issue with children of divorce, often carrying over into adulthood. This can affect many areas of one's life, including but not limited to dating and marital relationships, friendships, relationships with coworkers and supervisors, church relationships, and one's relationship with God. These effects are sometimes very apparent, but it is the more subtle effects that can be more detrimental. This is because the person is probably unaware that he is carrying scars from his parents' divorce, and because he is unaware, he's not likely to deal with the issues.

Respect goes hand-in-hand with trust as an issue. It is difficult, if not impossible, to respect someone you don't trust. When trust is compromised, so is respect.

Another impact of divorce is its often damaging effect on one's belief about commitment. When there is divorce, children see a lack of commitment from one or both parents. Divorce can become an acceptable option if marriage doesn't work out—an option that might not be considered if their parents had not divorced. I have heard clients say, "My parents divorced and I turned out OK!" But in reality, most of the time it's the effects of divorce that complicate their own relationships. Marriage isn't the only area that is affected by an impaired sense of commitment. Committing to a job, a church, a friendship, even a lease on an apartment can be affected.

It all ties back into trust as the core issue. When a person feels he was betrayed and abandoned as a child, its effect on trust can be debilitating. When trust has been compromised, so has respect and commitment. You cannot have healthy respect or commitment if you don't have trust. This core issue is where healing has to start!

Divorce damages relational equity. Let me describe how this plays out in a CMC:

Some people will have a perverted perspective of those who lead them. A person's greatest emotional impact comes from his or her parents. If either of the parents walked out on a group member at an early age, that member may retain underlying, even unrealized suspicion concerning the group leader. This group member may believe at some level that all leaders are unreliable and that "if I place my trust in the group's leader as I did my dad or mom, I will suffer emotional trauma again."

This will be especially true of an effective CMC leader who also fills the role of discipler. This role often mirrors the responsibilities given a parent as the leader nurtures, trains, teaches, holds accountable, and sometimes is called upon to lovingly redirect or discipline a group member.

Some will not make a wholehearted commitment to the group. Because Dad abandoned Mom (or vice versa) after agreeing to stay together for a lifetime (and did so through public wedding vows as well as a marriage license), it is subconsciously obvious to some children of divorced parents that no commitment must be kept. Commitment to relationships is lessened greatly when parents divorce.

A great leader will push back on the exiting group member and remind him or her that a CMC is a family and that a family member cannot just up and walk out on the rest of the family. But this statement cannot guarantee member loyalty, because it may mirror what the group member heard from his or her own parent before that parent walked out the door.

Some will leave the group rather than deal with conflict. When parents divorce, conflict is always part of the equation. Whether the conflict existed before some traumatic event or the traumatic event created the conflict, the child in the home of divorced parents most likely lived through conflictual moments. And what followed the conflict was the exit of a parent deeply loved and needed by the child. What has been modeled by the parent? When there is conflict, rather than stick around and deal with the issues that created the conflict, it's easier, even a sub-conscious necessity, to walk away from the relationship.

This becomes especially disastrous in small-group life because a healthy CMC will at some point experience conflict. When this happens, some of the members will, rather than do the hard work of working through the conflict and learning to make amends, leave the group. Because this was the path chosen by a parent, it is the response most natural to them.

At this point, I'm sure you're realizing that the actions and choices of people we respect the most have the power to greatly disturb the hearts of those in our CMCs. When they fall, we doubt; when they contradict their own principles, we begin to question the validity of those principles; when they model perverted values, we tend to instinctively follow their lead. And this is not just true when parents miss the mark. It's also true when pastors disregard the target completely.

LEADERS GONE BAD

Below you'll see two passages that outline requirements of pastors. Please read them slowly, underlining each of the qualities that are required of those who serve in the highest level of leadership.

The saying is trustworthy: If anyone aspires to the office of overseer, he desires a noble task. Therefore an overseer must be above reproach, the husband of one wife, sober-minded, self-controlled, respectable, hospitable, able to teach, not a drunkard, not violent but gentle, not quarrelsome, not a lover of money. He must manage his own household well, with all dignity keeping his children submissive, for if someone does not know how to manage his own household, how will he care for God's church? He must not be a recent convert, or he may become puffed up with conceit and fall into the condemnation of the devil. Moreover, he must be well thought of by outsiders, so that he may not fall into disgrace, into a snare of the devil. (1 Timothy 3:1-7)

This is why I left you in Crete, so that you might put what remained into order, and appoint elders in every town as I directed you — if anyone is above reproach, the husband of one wife, and his children are believers and not open to the charge of debauchery or insubordination. For an overseer, as God's steward, must be above reproach. He must not be arrogant or quick-tempered or a drunkard or violent or greedy for gain, but hospitable, a lover of good, self-controlled, upright, holy, and disciplined. He must hold firm to the trustworthy word as taught, so that he may be able to give instruction in sound doctrine and also to rebuke those who contradict it. (Titus 1:5-9)

Please go back and read each of the terms that you underlined one more time. Did you notice that most of the requirements for pastoring deal with character, consistency, and purity? Pastors are held to a very high standard. I believe we are held to such a high standard because our lives greatly impact the hearts and commitments of those we lead.

Quitting Church, a book written by Julia Duin to help us understand why people are leaving the local church, tells the story of Christine Scheller:

> Christine described a thirty-year period in her life of rotten ministers, starting when her pastor hit on her when she was eighteen. She managed to escape him unscathed, but the experience was light compared to another pastor who split the church, then had an affair with a church member. She recounts a succession of pastors who divorced, abused power, engaged in sexual sin, and otherwise betrayed the trust of their flock.[4]

Christine left the church. Why do people leave the church when pastors lack Christlikeness? They leave because their hearts are deeply affected. They say things like, "I just can't stand to be in the same room with him" or "My pastor will never know how much he hurt me" or "I could never trust the leadership of my pastor again." These are not words that flow from logic; they are phrases birthed in a broken and confused heart.

God gave pastors a role that has its greatest effect on the heart. Their influence can either build up or tear down. All too often pastors have not only broken the hearts of those they lead, they have broken into those hearts and stolen the influence of any Christian leader who will lead those people in the future.

Listen — when pastors lack integrity, some people will begin to question the authenticity of the God who called that pastor into service and the gospel that pastor has been proclaiming. When these people land in your CMC, you need to be aware that rebuilding their trust in leaders may take time, a lot of time.

JESUS IS BIG BUSINESS

As we continue to point out those things that landed us in the new reality, we can't overlook the commercialization of Jesus.

Any professional marketer will tell you "sex sells." Do you know why sex sells? Because it immediately catches everyone's attention. I tell you that "Jesus sells." Jesus sells because the name of Jesus and things connected to Christianity immediately catch the attention of a major demographic — those who call themselves Christians.

And because of this, Jesus is big business. Just stop by the lobby of your church to pay your teenager's fees to attend Christian camp or purchase a ticket to a Christian concert or conference. You'll pay extravagantly. If none of these opportunities rings your bell but you like to travel, you can choose from a long list of Christian bus tours, excursions to the Holy Land, or cruises designed for you to get to know your favorite preacher or singer up close and personal. Upon arrival at the concert or camp or while you're on any of the tours mentioned, you'll be introduced to "ancillary products." You can buy T-shirts, books, Bibles, even pictures of the personalities/stars you've come to hear sing, preach, keynote, or lead your small group at camp. Oftentimes these photographs have been "personally autographed."

Believe me, when the owners of these events, experiences, and ancillary products meet to discuss what you're going to pay, you can be sure they're not talking about "breaking even." The terms *margin*, *revenue*, and *profits* are almost always part of the conversation.

If Christian businesses continue to move further away from ministry and focus more on revenue, they find themselves doing whatever is necessary, within legal and ethical boundaries, to sell more product. And what is the strongest selling point to Christians? Jesus. The Jesus on the cross became the Jesus on the T-shirt. The Jesus of life-transforming worship became the Jesus of the $30 Christian concert ticket. The Jesus who had "nowhere to lay his head" (Matthew 8:20) became the Jesus whose story was written into songs that made a few Christian performers and publishing companies extravagant amounts of money.

As time has passed, even sincere believers often subconsciously adapt to the changing Christian culture. They are tempted to embrace the trite Jesus of the commercials rather than the unfathomable Jesus who created the universe, who came as God and lived among us, who healed the sick and raised the dead, who suffered the cruelest of deaths on the cross though He had never sinned, who rose on the third day — the Jesus who will return for His church someday to reign over His kingdom for all of eternity, and who sits at the right hand of God this very minute. This Jesus was diminished to being the Jesus of the slick slogan, the carefully chosen catchphrase, and the song hook.

When a CMC leader speaks Jesus' name, sometimes CMC members no longer revere Him. And in the loss of this reverence comes the loss of awe. But a sense of awe is what allows us to be transformed when in His presence.

THE SEEKER MENTALITY

Leadership consultant Dr. Bill Donahue served in the Group Life Ministry at Willow Creek during the zenith of the seeker movement. Reflecting on the movement, Bill says,

> The desire to connect with spiritual seekers by speaking their language and entering their culture (contextualization, like missionaries do in a foreign land or Paul did in Acts 17 on Mars Hill) was sometimes taken too far. Some churches that never grasped the heart and soul of the movement crossed the boundary line. They missed the *heart* of the seeker movement — creative expression of the gospel, the use of the arts, the focus on biblical themes and topics that people in the culture more readily understood, and the use of forms and architecture that seekers easily recognized. Instead they focused on the trappings — contemporary music, video, dress, buildings, programs — and made them the central focus. People thought if they substituted a rock band for a robed choir, spoke from a Plexiglas pulpit, dumbed down the gospel, and never mentioned sin, they were being "seeker friendly." And by doing so, many more visitors would show up.

The Western church was inadvertently establishing a dangerous ideal: Don't say anything that would create discomfort for a nonbeliever. As has been true in many eras, speaking the name of Jesus was difficult for people. No problem though. If church members would get seekers to weekend worship services, the teaching pastor would be certain they heard about Christ. Church members were now fully aware that it was their responsibility to bring people to the church.

Rather than elevate Jesus, church members elevated their church. They spoke of their cool pastor and his practical "talks," the awesome band and amazing singers, the state-of-the-art children's playland that "will make your kids want to come to church," and a "something for everyone" list of "opportunities" to choose from.

Don't get me wrong. I believe the seeker movement was vital for building bridges to lost people and for re-establishing corporate evangelism as a main emphasis at services. But in the process of becoming seeker sensitive, we unintentionally taught parishioners to sell their local church rather than share the story of their Christ. Most church leaders will quickly and vehemently argue that this was not so. We will even remind one another that we taught classes so that people in our churches would know how to voice the gospel.

But in the end, church members understood that their role was to build relationships and invite people to services. In some settings, Jesus' name became a secondary conversation. Not only that, the seeker-focused service took precedence over disciple-making. We were getting nonbelievers to the church, even in a relationship with Christ, but we were so focused on evangelizing that we overlooked the important role of the church to turn new believers into mature believers.

But it wasn't just the churches' accidental ecclesiastics that created heart tension; the sexual choices of an era also had its effects.

THE DAMAGE LEFT BY PROMISCUITY

Few experiences negatively influence the inner person as much as sexual encounters that contradict the guidelines given us by our Creator. Sexual experiences, once completed, cannot be undone. These irrevocable intimacies have intense and oftentimes subconscious negative effects on us and our relationships. Rick and Kathy Roepke, counselors with decades of experience, have said,

> Sexual sin has a definite effect on a person's psyche. For the Christian, conviction of sin is one effect. The more a person tries to squelch the conviction, the heavier it weighs on him or her, and can eventually lead to a hardened heart. It can also open the door for Satan to wreak havoc with guilt and shame, which then leads to lowered self-esteem, isolation and depression, and possibly self-medicating through drugs and/or alcohol. It could even lead to suicidal thoughts and actions, which would result in a psychiatric hospitalization or death.
>
> An increasingly common scenario in counseling involves one spouse who starts out viewing pornography. That sin leads to another—online chat sites with other people outside the marriage (emotional adultery). That sin leads to another—an actual adulterous relationship. The end result is a badly fractured marriage that might possibly end in divorce. Now, there are at least two main issues to deal with: the addiction to pornography and the fractured marriage. There will be multiple secondary issues as well.
>
> Regardless of the name of the sexual sin (adultery, pornography, homosexuality, premarital sex, etc.), choosing to invite it into our lives is like inviting a thief into our homes. It

robs us of love, joy, peace, happiness, self-confidence, and it ultimately distances us from God.

So established is the new sexual reality that teens today freely "hook up" before there is an emotional connection of any kind and bail without even considering the consequences. In his book *An Exposé on Teen Sex and Dating,* Andy Braner told of his conversation with a couple of teenagers: "One boy told me, 'At my school, when there is a dance coming up, a guy will text a girl to "hook up." (This is code for "Let's make out.") When they hook up, if everything goes as planned and they seem to like each other, then they might go to the dance together. It's all about how much they can do physically.'" In the next paragraph, a teen girl gives her perspective on sexuality: "At my school it's just understood that you have two weeks. You start hooking up, making out, having sex, and everyone knows in two weeks it will be over and you move on to someone else."[5]

But teens are just following the lead of those who have gone before them, their models, even their own parents.

What we have today is a system whereby a church, small group, or parachurch ministry might say, "Don't have sex before you get married—it's wrong." And all teens hear are rules and regulations. Whether or not there is an objective truth claim, they'll see it as subjective until they have real-life models who prove the rule is worth something. We can't continue to beat the drum of abstinence if we're not also willing to practice "till death do us part," model lifelong monogamy, and openly discuss the consequences in relationships where those commitments are valued. We have teens who are being quarantined because they're just doing what they see modeled in society. We watch teenagers who are overridden with guilt when they follow exactly what their elders have modeled.[6]

Every CMC leader must be aware that he or she leads group members in a society that seldom puts the sexual brakes on. From the private viewing of pornography to a one-nighter while on a business trip, some of the individuals in your group are most likely wrestling with the shame of, the guilt of, or the rationalization of a culturally acceptable sexual act.

At this point, you may be asking yourself why I've spent so much time describing the new realities, telling you what's happening in those realities, and how we arrived here. The reason is simple. All of the things mentioned to this point have been leading to what you are about to read.

I hope you can embrace these facts. The Norman Rockwell world is no more, and the planet you and I have been placed on is inhabited by individuals living by their own set of guidelines, the majority having set aside the Bible as their guide for life. Transient lifestyles are the norm, and they have a profound effect on the shaping of people's hearts and how they relate to the CMC they're in. Divorce is rampant and can greatly disturb how someone views life and leadership. Imperfect pastors and priests set the tone for cynicism when it comes to any group connected to a local church including small groups, how one views and responds to those placed in authority by the church, and who can be trusted. The commercialization of Jesus has diminished how He is viewed and has all but eclipsed the power of His holiness. Sexual activity outside the guidelines given us by God in Scripture has an insidious impact on the psyche and the believer's journey toward sanctification.

So what does it all mean to the people in your CMC? How

do these realities affect group members and group life? It has vandalized the environments where ultimate transformation takes place.

CHAPTER 3

REDEEMING VANDALIZED ENVIRONMENTS

Six environments have taken a major blow in the new reality. Look intently into each of them to see how they affect group members and the dynamic of your CMC. Getting a grip on each of them will help you understand what might be going on in the hearts of your group members.

RELIGION: SHEDDING INSTITUTIONAL BAGGAGE

In the minds of many, Christian institutions are the enemy. When Christ and His lifestyle are discussed, instinct tells everyone in the room that the church should reflect His character and should be and do what Jesus was and did. But when "the organized church" is brought into the conversation, the room turns cold very quickly.

Let's face it: Because many people do not understand the reasons behind some of the church's decisions, they don't see the church as exhibiting the personality of Jesus as well as she should. In many communities the church is seen as an ecclesiastical country club shrouded in church-speak looking out for her own self-interests. She uses her income to build workout centers and gymnasiums for the "membership" rather than feeding the poor. She is a people wholly welcoming only those already far down the road to perfection rather than being a community fully embracing those still wrestling with the sins that create catastrophic emotional trauma. She is a people unwilling to hold firmly to her beliefs as Jesus did and instead allows cultural norms to contradict even the directives of Jesus Himself. She is, when evaluated by many, an impotent, dysfunctional, self-centered organization, having lost her way, rather than being perceived as the living, caring, need-meeting, integrity-bearing image of Jesus Christ.

Instead of being a light on a hill administering the love of Christ, she is, in the minds of many, a self-perpetuating subculture bent on separation from and caring little about other groups.

When people choose to connect with a CMC, we need to remember that they bring with them the baggage of their church perspective. But more importantly, as they progress in shedding that baggage, they are willing to hold firmly to a people living like and loving like Christ.

INTIMACY: DISFIGURED HEARTS RESTORED BY GRACE

The emotional scars that were left by parents choosing their own selfish interests, the institutionalized church's tendency to run roughshod over the individual, and the individual's perverted sexuality—along with other sinful choices—have left the hearts of many people disfigured. Where they once felt a childlike innocence and beauty and were comfortable revealing their inner person, they now see ugliness inside themselves. They view their hearts as something to hide. The heart seems too disfigured to be brought out in the open. It is hideous and would bring shame if the world could see it.

So long have these persons hidden the perceived ugliness of their hearts that they have grown accustomed to keeping their real emotional self hidden. It is now instinctive to dodge a conversation that might demand an unveiling. And when others begin to take the veil off of their hearts, the heart-hidden soul silences the conversation lest he feel obligated to respond by revealing more of himself. This greatly hinders intimacy among group members because they experience intimacy as they reveal more than the facade they have created.

Each time a small group gathers, there is a room full of hearts longing to be brought out into the open. Some will be aggressive in revealing their true selves. But for many, opening up is more difficult than ever. Every small-group leader needs to remember that, over time, if he or she creates a safe enough environment through personal self-revelation, and if that grace-filled environment has been tested and proved to be a safe haven again and again, people will begin to unveil the parts of their hearts they see as ugly and distasteful. And, in time, Christ will redeem their hearts and the shame will be removed.

LEADERSHIP: TRUST BEGINS WITH FAITHFULNESS

Leadership is an earned opportunity. When someone proves to be a person of integrity and consistency and cares for others more than himself, he will earn enough respect to be given the right to lead others. Leadership is vital to any endeavor and especially a CMC.

But it is the heart of the follower that makes leading possible. A small-group leader may have leadership abilities and qualities, but until the small-group member's heart is open to trusting and giving over some of himself to the leader, the leader will not be able to lead that person. It is especially important to remember this as you lead groups today.

Many parents in this era have been quick to divorce, slow to put the child's needs before their own, and oftentimes unwilling to redeem the brokenness they have caused their now-adult children. Some pastors have been quick to teach, slow to follow their own teachings, and unable or unwilling to strive to reflect the character of Christ. Because God has given parents and pastors authority over a person's life, these two categories of leader especially have had a deep and debilitating negative effect.

The leader of a CMC should realize that it may take a very long time for some group members to allow him or her influence in their lives. This is because internal distrust is housed in their hearts. They will first have to see that the leader is not going to bail on them no matter what, that the leader welcomes them just as they are but is working in tandem with God to take them places they've never been before, and that the leader has their best interests in mind no matter what it costs.

CONFLICT: TRANSFORMATION COMES ONLY WITH HONESTY

Conflict is an often misunderstood aspect of group life. If a group is going to become all it can, conflict is essential. Only when people are honest with one another can transformation take place. Conflict often accompanies honesty because only when people are honest with one another is there something to be conflictual about.

But conflict is often misinterpreted as being an enemy of relationship. It is seen as an incapacitating abnormality and is interpreted as a danger that will ultimately end with the breakup of a group or relationship. This may be because many a person whose home was full of conflict was soon void of one parent or the other. They may believe, "When people experience conflict with one another, sooner or later one or the other exits." Instead of working out differences, the model for these people has been to run away from the conflict and the people of the conflict.

COMMITMENT: EXHIBITING THE CHARACTER OF CHRIST

Most healthy small groups agree to some specific expectations. This is what most group gurus call the small-group covenant. These commitments are what drive the group and create healthy boundaries. These agreements include expectations such as showing up on time for each gathering, participating during group meetings, and keeping things discussed in the group confidential.

For many group members, commitments of this nature are easily dismissed. Because we live in a society where keeping one's word is not nearly as important as enjoying one's life, agreements like this are thrown to the wayside without a second thought. Please don't misunderstand what I'm suggesting. When group members agree to these expectations, they really mean to keep their promises. But these agreements are easily undone. This is both a societal issue and a heart issue because society today puts less emphasis on character and more emphasis on one's personal agenda. It is a heart issue because, as a person is transformed into the image of Christ, his or her heart will begin to fall in line with the character of Christ. A CMC leader can't change society, but he or she can work with God to see someone's heart transformed.

Also, every group leader needs to understand that, due to lack of commitment many people make today, some will bail on a group for reasons mostly beyond the leader's control. Four are especially prominent and somewhat illogical:

- If a leader doesn't engage, impress, or encourage in the anticipated ways or as often as a group member would like, he may bail.
- If expectations seem too high, he may bail, even if he agreed to those expectations early in the group's life.
- If a better option comes along, he may bail even if the other option is playing on a softball team, bowling, or "I didn't realize *American Idol* was on the same night as small group."
- If friendships don't seem to form quickly enough, he will bail.

TRUTH: ALLOWING SCRIPTURE TO SPEAK

If a group reads the Bible together, truth will be expressed. Then the interpretation begins. It is during this phase of the conversation that truth will be concretely established, accidentally misdiagnosed, or completely ignored.

We must keep this one precarious fact in mind: Most people in today's world believe truth is relative. People with this bent start with a dangerous freedom. Their default is to conclude what God is saying by viewing Scripture through their own preexisting filters. For some, their filter is experience. What they have expe-rienced in the past determines how they will interpret God's words in the present. There are other misleading filters, including the psychological, the philosophical, and the scientific, which some will use as the starting point of interpretation. Please know that God may use these filters to prove His truth but the Enemy often uses them to confuse.

Group leaders must remember these two facts: (1) Many people do not believe that God is the only author of truth, so (2) conversations with group members must be carefully and delicately led so that everyone is heard and God's truth rises above all other opinions.

Yes, this vital environment of Scripture interpretation has been vandalized. But we can take the truth back if we are willing to diligently allow the truth of Scripture to speak for itself.

CHAPTER 4

CREATING HEALTHY TRIBAL CHRISTIAN MICRO-COMMUNITIES

Creating a tribal CMC is going to be one of the most exhilarating rides of your life. If you're like many of us, you have found yourself frustrated while leading groups. You are 100 percent sure that every small group must create an environment where a not-yet follower of Christ can hear, process, and accept the gospel, that the groups you lead move beyond just being friends to becoming fellow mature disciples, that every member realize how the Enemy is using his own story to hold him captive and how through Jesus' story he can be set free.

The problem: We have been using an old paradigm of group life in a new age. If we're going to effectively create transformational groups, we must consider some new ways of thinking and doing.

COMMON NECESSITIES

If we are going to create a transformational tribal community, we must lead our small groups into four necessities. These four necessities will create a unity of mind and spirit that will move a group from simply being a bunch of friends getting together for a Bible study to being a family swimming in the warm pool of transformational oneness. The four necessities are (1) a common language, (2) common memories, (3) common traditions, and (4) a common vision of community.

Common Language

Healthy communities share a common language. In this situation I don't mean Spanish or French or English. Common language is language that is known by a particular group and is understood by that group only. These are words and phrases that have significance to one specific community of people. In most cases, these words and phrases have been created by the group leader or a group member. Outsiders will understand the meaning of those words or phrases only when someone in the inner circle defines their meaning and explains their context and how they relate to one particular CMC.

These words and phrases can be strategically created or they can be spontaneous expressions that stick. Those that are strategically created are most often created by a leader. They take the form of a slogan, part of a purpose statement, or are a phrase passed down from the small-group pastor to every CMC for the purpose of keeping groups on the same page. For instance, one church I know uses these three words to describe what every small group and every group member is to be about: "Dinner, Discipleship, Discussion." When a new person joins a group, the small-group leader uses these three words to describe what the group does, tells him how these three expectations shape group life, and that he will be involved in "Dinner, Discipleship, and Discussion." The small-group pastor at this church strategically designated these three words. Only those who are part of a small group at the church truly understand the meaning of these words and then only because the meaning and context were explained to them.

But some of the most bonding common language in a small group is not strategically or purposefully created; rather, it is voiced in a humorous moment and sticks. These include pet names and, in most cases, funny phrases. I once arrived on a college campus to oversee a college ministry. Of course, the first thing I tried to do was meet everyone. I was introduced to Abe. Or at least I thought his name was Abe. I noticed that, when I was introduced to him, a few of the students in the room mischievously glanced and smirked at one another. Sometime later one of the students dialed me in. They told me that upon his arrival on campus, everyone thought he looked like Abraham Lincoln, so he was given the nickname of Abe. And because it was known only in that community, it had significance to them and bonded them together.

Then there are those phrases that stick. I was once leading a conference for small groups. A small group was seated around each table. I had asked each group to do an exercise. This one small group just kept laughing very loudly again and again and again. I strolled over to the table to see what was going on. Just as I got to the table, someone announced, "That's just dastardly." And once again the group went nuts with laughter. I asked them what the deal was. At some point in the group's experience together, someone had said, "That's just dastardly," and everyone laughed. Over time it became a signature phrase in the group. Anytime it's appropriate, and I can imagine sometimes when it's not, when someone says the phrase, everyone in the group responds because they know the phrase and its context. The group owns the phrase, and it bonds and sets the members of the group aside as those who exclusively own and use it.

Where there is a common language, there is a common bond.

Common Memories

Common memories are snapshots of moments in time that have been shared by a group of people, in this situation, a CMC. It could be the mental image of someone in the group hugging a homeless man while serving with the group at a soup kitchen. It's the mental image of a group member stumbling, trying to catch himself, and falling while the group was hiking together. It's the mental rerun of two group members consoling one another following the death of a family member. It's the mental replay of the group so overcome by laughter that one group member sprints to the bathroom while another is laughing so hard she is crying.

A small group takes a giant leap toward becoming a tightly knit community when it shares common memories. Common memories happen when groups do life and ministry together. A CMC leader doesn't need to plan to create common memories; he or she needs only create an environment where people experience life together and carry out the mission of Christ together. Common memories will follow.

Common Traditions

In the Old Testament, God Himself designated dates and assigned expectations for celebrations and rituals. In so doing He consistently reminded His people of His love for them, His covenant with them, and His willingness to bless them. In the New Testament, Jesus commanded His people to partake of the Lord's Supper so that they would not forget His love for them and so they would revel in the beauty and power of the gospel.

Another important purpose is served when a group of people establishes common traditions—a healthy community is formed. In order for a small group to become more than just friends, it is vital for the group to establish common and consistent traditions.

These traditions could be anything from having a meal before each meeting to going on a mission trip together every July. The group might do its annual Christmas party with a White Elephant gift exchange or go to the lake together each summer before school starts.

It's best to establish common traditions that occur weekly, monthly, seasonally, and annually. When thinking of a weekly tradition, think of your CMC meeting. This can be as trite as having snacks each week at the end of the meeting or as significant as partaking of the Lord's Supper together. When considering a monthly tradition think of your group's schedules and needs. If your group is made up of young couples with children, you might want to cancel your regular meeting once a month, making it possible for each couple to have a date night. Or, if your group serves snacks only on a regular meeting night, once a month you might want to have a full meal together. Maybe your group is very missional, so you'll want to consider once a month taking on a mission endeavor of some kind. Seasonal traditions may be driven by the weather during a given season or the sport that is most prominent. For instance, a small group may choose to go snow skiing in the winter, attend a marriage conference together in the spring, go fishing together in the summer, and hike together in the fall. Planning common traditions during sporting seasons is not unusual either. You'd be amazed at how many small groups have an annual Super Bowl party, create a contest around the NCAA Final Four basketball extravaganza, or travel to see their favorite college football team play their most bitter rivals. Annual traditions are wisely created to coincide with major holidays.

Common traditions are vital also because they bring a sense of stability to individuals in a small group. The level of growth in a person's life is directly related to how secure he feels with the other people he is journeying with. For many, the first time they will experience common traditions that create a sense of stability, oneness, and family will be in their CMC.

Having grown up in either one-parent homes or homes whose daily routine was governed by baseball games, dance practices, Mom and Dad's busy lifestyles, maybe even over-involvement in church activities, many CMC members have never experienced the power of common traditions. When adults arrive in your small group, their hearts are subconsciously longing for established and consistent traditions. If you will create them and be consistent in doing them, you have done much in creating a sense of security for your group members and in building a healthy community.

Common Vision of Community

Maybe the most important common necessity is a vision of Christian community. When someone joins a group, he or she has some expectation of what the group will be and do, what the environment will look like when the group has known one another for a long time, and how the group will function. And oftentimes, each group member has a different image in mind. For some, a Christian community is primarily about building great friendships. Someone else may be anticipating the group to be a support group giving most of its time to listening to one another, giving wise counsel to one another, and making room for long conversations based on the needs of the group members. Someone else may enter the group believing it will focus on deep discipleship, that Scripture will be memorized, entire books of the Bible read each week, and hours spent in meditation between meetings. As you can see, there can be many visions when someone says "small group."

Until the leader or the entire CMC, through discussion and agreement, determines what the primary vision for the group is, the group's identity will never be established. Each person will bring his own flavor to the group experience, believing he is living out what the group is about. The person who believed the group was a support group will come with story in hand, ready to unveil her pain to the group. The person who thought the group was going to "make real disciples" will be disturbed that there aren't others in the group spending substantial amounts of time in the Word weekly and ready to be held accountable for Scripture memorization. The individuals who assumed the group was going to be a laid-back gathering of others just needing some Christian friends will be disturbed, even angry, when homework is discussed.

A group without an agreed-upon vision will struggle. It will never realize its group identity, meaning it will continue at some level in "group schizophrenia," never knowing who it really is. But more devastating than this, it may never be a unified family exhibiting the love and unity that is magnetic to those who have either turned their backs on Christ or never started a relationship with Him.

DISCONNECT THE INSTITUTIONAL CHURCH FROM THE GATHERING

Your small group is most likely sponsored by a local church, but if you're going to reach people far from Christ and regather those who have walked away from Him and His church, you may have to downplay that fact.

The local church is suspect in the minds of many. If you mingle with any people other than church members—and they are honest with you—you will not be blindsided when you remember that many people see the church as irrelevant, only after people's money, and a big waste of time. You might be surprised to find out that there's more to it even than this. David Kinnaman's book *Unchristian* shares these astounding words:

> Our research shows that many of those outside Christianity, especially younger adults, have little trust in the Christian faith, and esteem for the lifestyle of Christ followers is quickly fading among outsiders. They admit their emotional and intellectual barriers go up when they are around Christians, and they reject Jesus because they feel rejected by Christians.[1]

Kinnaman went on to tell us the issues that create this tension:

> In our national surveys with young people, we found the three most common perceptions of present-day Christianity are anti-homosexual (an image held by 91 percent of young outsiders), judgmental (87 percent), and hypocritical (85 percent). These "big three" are followed by additional negative perceptions, embraced by a majority of young adults: old-fashioned, too involved in politics, out of touch with reality, insensitive to others, boring, not accepting of other faiths, and confusing.[2]

George Barna estimates the number of unchurched Americans is growing by about 1 million per year. We have got to grasp reality—the institutional church has a reputation problem.

For those of us who have a deep love for "the church down the street" and long to see it grow, we must set aside the emotions that are welling up in us now and look purposefully into the eyes of reality. If we invite people to join our group who not only doubt the credibility of the church but are angry with her and we feel obligated to announce the name of the church that sponsors our group, we may never see the transformation in their lives we long for. They will never consider becoming part of our group, which means they may never reap the benefits of the small Christ-centered group that is our CMC.

You show no lack of commitment to Christ or your church if you welcome people to the gathering of your group without speaking of the group's connection to a larger body, an institutional church. There is no wrongness in realizing that your ultimate goal is to make disciples, not church members. And you are not dishonoring your local church if you are wise enough to meet those who are far from Christ or disconnected from the body of Christ and direct them on the next step of their journey. Remember this: A small-group leader in a tribal CMC is first and foremost an ambassador for Christ.

RETREAT FROM OLD LINES OF AUTHORITY

As a CMC leader leads a tribal group, he should keep in mind that his tribe views the church chain of command differently than in the past. In the old Rockwellian paradigm, the lines of authority looked something like this:

- The Bible was the ultimate authority on all matters.
- Next on the flowchart of credibility was the senior pastor.
- After the pastor came the church. Once a vote was taken by the church body, the decision was final.

- And finally, the small group or Sunday school class could speak into the issue.

This has changed. Because personal relationship now trumps the organizational structure and because the clergy are not as respected as they once were:

- The small group will have the most impact on a person's thoughts and actions.
- Next in line will be the larger body of believers, a local church.
- The Bible will speak into one's life.
- And finally, the senior pastor will then be given a hearing.

Please don't misunderstand: I am not suggesting that this is how it should be or that every person sees the influencer flowchart in this way. I am saying that the pendulum has swung in a new direction and we must respond. What does this mean to a tribal CMC leader?

The CMC leader has, in comparison to other leaders, much more credibility and thus much more responsibility than in the past. A tribal small-group leader must be willing to:

- Shepherd, not just lead
- Learn, teach, and protect sound doctrine
- Instill in group members' minds and hearts that those who make up their local church are important and that the larger body of believers is by God's design
- Help group members understand the role of pastors and the respect and honor that they deserve

- Elevate Scripture so that every group member drives each other to God's Word for the answers to all of life's questions, doctrinal understandings, and the gospel

In the new paradigm of group life, a CMC leader may have more respect given him than any other person in the church body. It is vital to the kingdom, not just the church or his small group, that he use his influence well.

PRACTICE TRIBAL LEADERSHIP

In a tribal small group, the leader subtly drives the group to be and do New Testament life together. The leader has a vital and complex role: moving the group away from societal norms and guiding the group to be a biblical community. For many small-group members, because they are "old infants" in their journey with Christ or they are simply carnal, living as though they had never become a follower of Jesus, a new paradigm of doing life together will be especially difficult.

Doing what comes naturally is always the default, especially when it comes to relationships. And what is natural to young and carnal believers relationally is looking out for the emotional health of number one. Biblical community is just the opposite—it demands setting self aside and looking out for the best inter-est of everyone else. These contradictory paradigms make the small-group leader's role especially important as he or she is the key factor in helping small-group members rethink and retool the way they live their lives.

The small-group leader must create an environment where the group is doing the Christian life together as designed by God and outlined in Scripture. When this happens, the small group will be a place so safe you will see the calling out of one another when sin in someone's life is noticed, the confessing of sin to one another so that prayers of godly brothers and sisters in Christ can be voiced, the requesting of financial or emotional assistance when it is needed, and the telling of one's story even if it includes abuse, acts of sexual perversion, addiction, or any other long-held secret.

This degree of safety will demand . . .

- Honesty, which demands . . .
- Trust, which demands . . .
- Communal understandings, which demand . . .
- Commitment, which demands . . .
- Sacrifice, which demands . . .
- A community of individuals willing to die for one another.

If you look again at the list above, you'll see that the environment a small-group leader desires all begins with a willingness to die for one another. Let me trace the progression. When a group member is willing to die for the others in the group, that person is willing to make *sacrifices* on behalf of the others. These sacrifices demand a *commitment* to the persons in the group. The necessary commitment cannot be realized until there are *communal understandings*. In the small-group setting this would be the biblical mandates concerning how to do life together. Communal understandings are what make it possible to *trust* one another as all of us will be committed to the same relational principles and expectations. And once we trust one another, we'll be able to be *honest* with one another, making it possible for the group to be bold in opening themselves up to one another.

We shouldn't be surprised that Jesus said, "This is my commandment, that you love one another as I have loved you. Greater love has no one than this, that someone lay down his life for his friends" (John 15:12-13). We shouldn't be surprised that a willingness to set aside self and give your life to others is the key to living in authentic, life-transforming community.

Before any of this can be realized, the small-group leader must be willing to revisit his or her leadership style. Many of those in groups today have a subconscious disdain for leaders because the leaders who impact the heart more than any others created an undeniable inner tension when it comes to trusting and following other leaders. Dad walked out on Mom or vice versa. The pastor a small-group member admired and learned from left the church due to an extramarital affair. The list goes on and on. The question has become, "Can leaders be trusted or will they at some point walk out on those they lead or contradict everything they once stood for?" This creates a great and sometimes unacknowledged tension for group members, a tension that will demand the leader of the group rebuild a leadership trust. It is for this reason that the small-group leader must:

- Be more of a *co-laborer* with the leadership role than the *manager* of a team
- Be more of a *nurturer* than a *teacher*
- Be more of a *consensus encourager* than an *autocrat*

And the leader must:

- Be willing to *earn influence* rather than depend on *title* to grant *influence*

Bottom line: The leader must lead from a heart saturated in humility. When a leader does this, he or she will reflect the attitudes and actions of Christ without being void of authenticity. This is the only way to be seen as lacking a hypocritical nature, which is the death of a Christian leader today.

Many small-group leaders will be asking, "How can I be and do all that is outlined here?" Actually, it's very simple and, well . . . Jesus-like. When Jesus was prompted to identify the greatest commandment, He said, "'And you shall love the Lord your God with all your heart and with all your soul and with all your mind and with all your strength.' The second is this: 'You shall love your neighbor as yourself.' There is no other commandment greater than these" (Mark 12:30-31). Small-group leaders should notice that in taking their eyes off themselves, they will carry out the greatest expectation given to humankind. They will also have a flourishing CMC.

Jim Egli and Dwight Marable surveyed more than three thousand small-group leaders in twenty-one countries.[3] Their research led them to this conclusion:

> Having surveyed thousands of small group leaders and analyzed hundreds of thousands of data points, in a word we can say that the one critical factor to having a vibrant growing small group is relationship—relationship with God and relationship with others. Growing groups have leaders who are connected to God and empowering others.[4]

ELIMINATE THE BOXES

Freedom is an instinctive expectation, a longing placed by God in the human heart. At times we may be forced into ideological boxes that make our hearts cringe and hinder us from breathing the fresh air of what is right. However, we are followers of Christ, and because of this our ideological understandings are in place. God's guidelines were given to us in Scripture. We choose to embrace them because they are ultimate freedom to us. We don't consider these expectations another box we're held captive in. A mature Christ follower realizes that turning our back on God's guidelines will lead to our being held in an even more confining captivity.

But what happens to the heart when God's requirements are added onto by denominational leaders, church leaders, family members, peers, or perceived expectations of a Christian community? The outcome is more bondage rather than more freedom.

Leading a small group today demands we recognize the boxes that are holding CMC members captive. Why? (1) The only way they will be set free is if a CMC leader knows what those boxes are and aids in freeing the small-group member being held captive. (2) Because we live in an age of very attainable information, many small-group members will realize that some expectations are heaped upon them by someone other than God and rebellion will rear its ugly head. And (3) when a CMC discusses some issues, small-group members may push back hard, and sometimes they should.

Five boxes are prevalent today: the denominational box, the local church box, the moral code box, the cultural Christian box, and the family lineage box.

The Denominational Box

The denominational box is built each time a denomination sets out an understanding of Scripture that contradicts, adds to, or tweaks what the Bible really says. In most instances these denominational ideals are couched in the term *denominational distinctives*. That is, expectations, guidelines, or doctrinal ideas considered distinctive to that one group of believers. For instance, many major denominations have declared the partaking of any alcoholic beverage at any level to be wrong, yet most pastors of those denominations would agree that Scripture speaks only of drinking alcohol to the point of drunkenness to be sinful activity.

The problem with denominational distinctives in this era is that small-group members are no longer striving to be good Methodists or Lutherans or Baptists. CMC members who are longing to be in right relationship with God and doing what it takes to become mature followers are pursuing the goal of becoming biblically functioning followers of Christ. And if any denominational distinctive contradicts what is scriptural, those believers will choose truth over denominational distinctive every time. Not only that, they will continue to become more suspect of church leaders, churches, and denominations.

The Local Church Box

The local church box is built each time a local church creates stated or unstated expectations for members, expectations that go beyond the Bible. This box has a profound effect on those who attend that church. Because those making decisions for a particular body of believers are often in close-knit relationships with those they are making decisions for, a declaration that hits home can wound the church member deeply and often drive a stake even deeper into the heart of the individual who is pointed out or who questions the trumped-up expectation.

For instance, I remember talking with a small-group leader

after a conference I had led. The leader was heartbroken that her young-adult son had declared he would never go back to church again, ever. The church leadership in their small rural church had gone down a path toward a more contemporary worship style. For a period, the church had a band that led worship on Sunday mornings. After the ouster of the lead pastor, the church took a vote and drums would never be allowed in that church again. Some had even publically declared that drums were satanic. This small-group leader's son was the drummer.

But it's not just issues of this nature that are box builders. Even membership requirements that are beyond biblical expectations can throw someone into the local church box. And when this happens, some are then driven to probe the edges of insanity for an escape route. I once bought a truck from a man who attended a church whose pastor announced that God had told him that every household was to give $3,000 to the building program. Here's what happened: As this young believer and I were talking about the truck, he asked what I did for a living. I told him I had been in ministry throughout my adult life. He asked me, "Is it right for a pastor to tell each church member how much to give to a building program? My wife and I already tithe."

When local church boxes are built and people are forced into them, the levels of bondage are overwhelming. Individuals forced into these boxes carry heavy loads placed on them by those who mean well but miss the mark. Many a Christian counselor has spent multiple sessions with someone who has been forced into the local church box because what is often determined to be "an important addition to the constitution and by-laws" is actually a passive form of spiritual abuse.

The Moral Code Box

The moral code box is created each time a moral code that is beyond biblical expectation is assigned by any religious authority. This could be a denomination, a local church, even a small-group leader. The moral code box is confining and even spiritually debilitating because it sets legalism as the default when determining how one should live one's life. Issues such as going to movies, how much money someone should keep for himself when there are poor people in the community, or what television shows are suitable for viewing all fit into the moral code box.

When the moral code discussion rears its head during a small-group discussion, these waters get very muddy and can create a tension that can lead to devastating conflict. Every CMC leader needs to be aware of these boxes and must be certain he doesn't impose his moral code on the group members he leads or allow group members to impose their code on others.

The Cultural Christian Box

If you've been a churchgoer for any length of time, you instinctively know the cultural Christian box. This box overflows with expectations created mostly by those who seldom mingle with those outside the faith. Expectations in the cultural Christian box may be directives that over time were embraced and thought of as biblical expressions. Examples often seen in southern U.S. churches include attending Sunday night worship services, reading only the King James Version Bible, and dressing up for church services.

But often, things in this category aren't expectations, they're attitudes—for instance, passive-aggressive behavior or ignoring a fellow Christ follower who said something hurtful rather than going to him or her to point out the statement and reconcile. The attitudes that drive these actions contradict Scripture but they are not only accepted, they are culturally normal. They are culturally Christian and undoubtedly contradictory to the teachings of Jesus.

The Family Lineage Box

The family lineage box has been in play from the day you were born. Realizing this box exists and that it may have the most positive or negative effects on one's heart is vital to the transformation of CMC members. The family lineage box holds attitudes and actions put there by the family members who influenced us. Experiences, expectations, and statements that shaped us are what cram us into the family lineage box.

Dan B. Allender put it like this: "The cast is sometimes obvious—our parents, siblings, spouse, mentors, abusers, and friends. But sometimes an important role is played by a grandparent we barely knew or a person, a family secret, who stands in the shadows offstage. We are defined by the people in our life."[5]

The family lineage box is filled with statements such as "Men never cry or talk about their feelings," "We don't ever discuss what goes on in this house with anyone," or "Never talk about religion or politics." But the family lineage box may also include things as trite as how to dress for church.

Family lineage boxes hold many small-group members captive forever. No box has a grip on us like this one because no other box is as able to demand our silence lest we hurt those who love us the most. We believe they may never love us again if we step outside the box or reveal its secrets.

STOP PROTECTING THE BRAND

In business, a company must protect its brand—what sets the company or product apart from all others. Denominations and churches do the same. They may not call it protecting the brand, they may not even realize they are doing it, but they are protecting their brand nevertheless.

In the world of religion, brands are usually established and protected in a certain way: First, a denomination or church through a political process determines a doctrinal bottom line, its style of worship, where it stands on controversial issues, whether or not it will do expository or topical preaching, and more. This could have been decided by senior leadership, a committee, a congregational vote, or a vote by denominational leaders, but a conclusion is reached. That conclusion is then made known to the larger body. The majority, even the masses, fall in line with that expectation. Over time the denomination or congregation is known for its perspective on a certain issue. At that point, the stance is part of the organization's brand. It sets it apart from most others. And once something is part of an organization's brand, it is difficult to abandon.

For example, let's return to an issue discussed earlier: avoiding alcoholic beverages. A few denominations have made this part of their brand. They have for decades held to this ideal firmly. Even most pastors in these denominations realize what Scripture says—that if someone doesn't drink to the point of drunkenness, there is no sin in it—but they hold to this belief anyway.

When a CMC meets, the leader must stop protecting the brand and allow God's Word to speak for itself. In the world in which we live and lead, people have access to information as never before. They are vividly aware of religious stances that are brand-specific and not biblically grounded.

The brand isn't nearly as important as the truth, and each time we protect the brand instead of helping our group members embrace biblical reality, they lose a little respect for us as group leaders as well as the church and denomination that holds so firmly to that which simply isn't stated in Scripture.

PRACTICE MYSTICAL MEANDERING

When God does something unexplainable, unfathomable, undeniably something only He could do, people take notice. They realize that Jesus is who He said He is, the Son of God. Calvin Miller pointed out: "Thomas the Doubter didn't believe the resurrection until he actually saw the Lord alive again. Yet when he saw the living Christ, he didn't say, 'Oh, now I see.' What he came to believe was not the miracle itself but the Christ behind the miracle."[6]

We're comfortable letting our small groups experience Jesus' many dimensions: Jesus the teacher, Jesus the consoler, Jesus the need-meeter, and Jesus the sacrificial Lamb are all espoused in group life. However, Jesus the producer of the miraculous is taught but seldom acted upon. Should it be? I believe we must practice mystical meandering. That is, wandering into the presence and power of God, allowing Him to work as He chooses.

The greatest reason for mystical meandering is so that group members can believe and embrace the gospel. Wayne Grudem wrote, "One purpose of miracles is certainly to authenticate the message of the gospel. This was evident in Jesus' own ministry, as people like Nicodemus acknowledged: 'We know that you are a teacher come from God; for no one can do these signs that you do unless God is with him' (John 3:2)."[7] Grudem continued, "When miracles occur, they give evidence that God is truly at work and so serve to advance the gospel: the Samaritan woman proclaimed to her village, 'Come, see a man who told me all that I ever did' (John 4:29), and many of the Samaritans believed in Christ."[8]

Is it possible that small groups today are far from fully recognizing the power of the gospel because members are not being led to recognize the power of Jesus? While Jesus is capable of the miraculous, it seems the church is incapable of offering Him the opportunity. Some are bailing on the church because in many cases she has abandoned a potent faith. Lori Rentzel chose churchlessness rather than settling for a church life void of a powerful Jesus. Julia Duin recorded some of Lori's spiritual history:

> Lori Rentzel, a churchless Christian in Petaluma, California, told me of her early days as a believer at the Open Door, a church she attended in the 1970s. Hers was a Pentecostal Christian culture where it was considered natural to cast out demons, engage in spiritual warfare, or pray for supernatural healing, sometimes all in one morning. "Those were the days when you never wanted to miss church because so much was going on," she said. "I had my first child on a Tuesday and I was in church that next Sunday. That was the kind of place it was." Rentzel went on to say, "Church seems to be a preset mold and you either fit into it or not. I want to go back. But it takes a lot of effort after working all week and doing errands all Saturday. And if you do go, you want something back. You need your batteries charged. Open Door was like that. But church is not like that anymore. You get no return for what you put into it."[9]

One of my own family members had abandoned church. He and his wife had been good church attendees their whole lives. They had consistently been involved with good Bible-teaching churches throughout their marriage. But something was missing. He had read the biblical accounts over and over again and believed a dimension to church life was being overlooked. He was seeing the book of Acts taught but never lived out. He left church and told his wife he would return only if they found a church where God was "doing something." They did. He and his family are now in a church that believes in the power of God, requests that God accomplish what only He is capable of accomplishing, and gives God the glory when He does.

Before you throw this book against the wall, realize this: Mystical meandering doesn't mean that a small group schedules its meeting time to coincide with the latest televised Benny Hinn crusade. It does mean that when an issue arises or a need is evident, the group considers doing what is natural and biblical—crying out to God, asking Him to act, believing He will, and if He doesn't respond in the way that was requested, giving Him glory for answering the requests as He saw fit, in His sovereign will.

It is natural to do this. When a need is voiced, calling out to the One who can meet that need, especially when God is the only One who is able, is the natural thing to do. And it is biblical. I am amazed that when I talk to people about the concept of mystical meandering, many of them, mostly pastors, look at me as if I need to seek a good Christian counselor. If I can talk with them, I quickly realize that they are hesitant. This amazes me. If we are reading and studying the Bible daily, more often than not, we encounter something unexplainable God did, a miracle Jesus performed, or something undeniable the apostles accomplished in the name of Jesus. It seems we would be so saturated in these stories that the extraordinary would spill over into our ordinary world, that our first thought would be to anticipate God's willingness to consider our requests.

Making mystical meandering a common practice will change the timbre of a small group. Mystical meandering unifies a small group as members make passionate requests of God together. Mystical meandering turns a group's eyes away from self and onto God. Mystical meandering helps a group make its primary goal to glorify God. Mystical meandering is a surefire way to let unbelievers see that believers believe. Mystical meandering intertwines our stories and Jesus' story at the deepest level. Mystical meandering makes the Bible more than just a book of long-ago stories; it comes alive as the story of stories that is no longer far away becomes our story in the present, and Jesus is with us once again in our world doing what only He can do.

Let's face it—a small group willing to meander into these sacred places with humble hearts will experience a dimension of group life and Jesus that is truly transforming.[10]

BE DOING COMMUNITIES

Most small groups do well at being relational communities. Some are really effective when it comes to being teaching communities. And I'm thrilled to say that many are becoming "doing" communities. That is, they are giving major attention and time to being missional together.

This is vital. From Jesus' time to now, doing—not just gathering—has been the responsibility of those who call themselves followers of Christ. In AD 30-something, Jesus announced,

> You are the salt of the earth, but if salt has lost its taste, how shall its saltiness be restored? It is no longer good for anything except to be thrown out and trampled under people's feet. You are the light of the world. A city set on a hill cannot be hidden. Nor do people

light a lamp and put it under a basket, but on a stand, and it gives light to all in the house. In the same way, let your light shine before others, so that they may *see your good works* and give glory to your Father who is in heaven. (Matthew 5:13-16, emphasis added)

It is in the *doing of good works* that Jesus' light shines brightest through a CMC.

Luke said this about the early church:

And they devoted themselves to the apostles' teaching and the fellowship, to the breaking of bread and the prayers. And awe came upon every soul, and many wonders and signs were being done through the apostles. And all who believed were together and had all things in common. And they were selling their possessions and belongings and distributing the proceeds to all, as any had need. And day by day, attending the temple together and breaking bread in their homes, they received their food with glad and generous hearts, praising God and having favor with all the people. And the Lord added to their number day by day those who were being saved. (Acts 2:42-47)

After the Holy Spirit came upon the church, she was in the community and "many wonders and signs were being done through the apostles." The believers were "selling their possessions and belongings and distributing the proceeds to all, as any had need." Jesus' words in Matthew 5 were proved true—when the church was salty and illuminating, "the Lord added to their number day by day those who were being saved."

Being a doing community is a key to having a balanced and healthy CMC, but more importantly, in a world where Christianity is questioned at every turn, it may be the primary entry point into the hearts of those who are far from Christ and proud of it.

CONSIDER INTERGENERATIONAL GROUPS

Most churches have created churches within a church. They have a children's church, a youth church, a young adult church, and a senior adult church—all in one church. In wanting to create the right learning environment for each age group, they have, in the process, created four different churches. In many larger churches, each of these age groups has its own logo, purpose statement, core values, small-group system, even its own worship service with its own age-appropriate music and pulpiteer. While there is nothing wrong in this, it may be that the small-group ministry would be wise to reconsider age-graded grouping and replace that with intergenerational groups.

Okay, before I go any further, I realize I'm about to tread on less-than-thin ice. In fact, I already sense that for many of you, I've already broken through and am drowning in the cold waters of your discontent, maybe even anger. I understand. But I don't believe we can ignore some important facts.

Fact #1: Discipleship Is More Relational Than Informational

Churches organize members by age group because the goal is to instill information. Educators have wisely pointed out that preschoolers learn and retain information in a way that is distinctive to their age group. Children in elementary school have a different way of learning and are able to understand and embrace different and larger amounts of information than preschoolers. Middle school kids have their own bent when it comes to learning and retaining information, and high schoolers differ from middle schoolers. Because instilling information was the goal, the obvious choice was to group by age.

But what if the ultimate goal isn't knowledge? Our ultimate goal is to make mature disciples, not biblical scholars. And discipleship is more relational than informational. George Barna understands this principle and proved it when he described the discipling process. He wrote,

> In the original biblical texts, the term used for disciple refers to someone who is a learner or follower, serving as an apprentice under the tutelage of a master. The apostles are great examples of this relationship between a student and master: they followed Jesus, the master teacher and model of the Christian faith, striving to learn from His words and deeds, growing through the practical hands-on training that He facilitated.[11]

Mature disciples are made not only in a classroom but in a home, on the ball field, on the mission field, while playing a game, or while building a garage. Disciples are made when a less mature believer is in relationship with a more mature believer, watching how he responds to difficult life situations, listening to him when he points out a biblical truth or talks with someone far from Christ, learning from him as he speaks wisdom from God's Word, and as he journeys alongside the growing believer—being aware that the discipler is further along in his journey than the disciple is.

Don't misunderstand me: Learning God's Word is vital to anyone's journey with Christ, and attending classes where the Bible is taught is important. But mature disciples are not made in a classroom; they are made as people walk alongside one another and as the disciple does what he or she has seen done. Discipleship takes place not only when one is being taught but mostly when one is walking alongside, watching, processing, and practicing what the discipler is teaching, being, and doing.

You know where I'm headed and I think I know what you're thinking: You don't have to be older to be more spiritually mature. I agree wholeheartedly, but in most instances this will be true. Someone who has had more years studying and living God's expectations, more opportunities to process life through the lenses of Scripture, more struggles and suffering with sin issues, who has practiced the spiritual disciplines longer, will in most instances be more mature and adept in leading another believer toward greater spiritual maturity than a peer. Think about it: Do we really think that a sixteen-year-old boy in a Sunday school class with other sixteen-year-old boys is going to be more effectively discipled than if he is spending time with the mature adult men in his inter-generational small group? Do we really believe that the twenty-something mom will gain greater wisdom concerning biblical parenting by being discipled by another first-time mom of the same age or a fiftysomething on the other side of the parenting process?

Intergenerational groups allow group members to journey with people who have already been where they are, whether on the practical or the spiritual front.

Fact #2: Intergenerational Groups Require Moms and Dads to Be Models and Mentors

George Barna reported,

> Parents across the nation admit that one of the greatest benefits they receive from attending a church is having that community

of faith assume responsibility for the spiritual development of their children. Our national surveys have shown that while more than 4 out of 5 parents (85 percent) believe they have the primary responsibility for the moral and spiritual development of their children, more than two out of three abdicate that responsibility to their church.[12]

The first intergenerational small-group meeting our family attended was also a deafening wake-up call. My youngest son, who was sixteen and on a path far from God at the time, attended with us. As we were leaving, he pointed out that he had never seen me spend time with my Christian peers. That is, he had never seen his mom and me in an organized setting with a small group of fellow Christ followers where we were talking about our journey with Christ, encouraging other believers, praying for our friends, or, through discussion, seeking to find out what the Bible was unveiling to the group. The bottom line—because he had been in age-graded learning experiences his entire life, his parents had not had the chance to model how adults do the Christian life together.

If you had asked him who his spiritual model or mentor was, he would have said it was his youth small-group leader. Don't miss this: The person leading or who is most prominent in the organized and sanctioned church programs that a Christian teenager attends will naturally be viewed by that teen as the most influential person in his or her faith journey. It might be a Sunday school teacher or it might be the youth pastor. But seldom will a teen say it is his mom or dad.

The problem: Scripture blatantly and unapologetically points out that parents should be the primary models and spiritual mentors for their children.

A healthy intergenerational small group is the perfect place for a child to see a multidimensional Christian life modeled by Mom and Dad. A great group will cry out to God on behalf of one another, be on mission together, learn and live out God's directives found in Scripture together, carry one another's burdens, forgive one another, and so forth.

Some will say that the same modeling can occur when a really effective small-group leader leads a group of youth to do these things. This is just not so. For some reason beyond human comprehension, God designed the human heart in such a way that a child's parents will have the greatest influence on the child's future behavior. No one can take the parents' position in a child's life.

Intergenerational groups make it possible for Mom and Dad to be the primary models and mentors for their children, as God designed it to be.

Fact #3: Intergenerational Small Groups Are the Key to the Next Generation Continuing to Connect with a Local Church

Statistics have proved that "five or more" adults investing time with a teen "personally and spiritually" is a vital factor in a youth's continuing to journey with a local church.

"Teens who had at least one adult from church make a significant time investment in their lives also were more likely to keep attending church. More of those who stayed in church — by a margin of 46 percent to 28 percent — said five or more adults at church had invested time with them personally and spiritually."[13]

There may be no more natural way for a teen to be substantially connected to five adults who invest in him personally and spiritually than by his being involved in an intergenerational small group.

Not only does an intergenerational small group place teens in geographical closeness, it also places the hearts of several believing adults close to every teen in the group. Teens involved in an intergenerational small group will experience not only the teachings of one adult they respect, which they would gain if they were part of an age-graded small group or Sunday school class led by an adult, but they will also encounter the tutelage, lifestyles, spiritual awareness, and wise counsel of at least five adults in an intergenerational small group.

Fact #4: Young Adults Long For and Need Older Adults to Mentor Them

In 2005, LifeWay Christian Resources did an extensive study of young adults. Their interviews pointed out the following facts:

- Young adults are looking for deep, family-like relationships.[14]
- Young adults have a strong desire for relationships with people who are more experienced at life.
- Young adults have an increased interest in learning from other people's mistakes and experiences.
- Young adults have a desire for relationships that go beyond their own stages of life.
- Young adults have a general longing for older companionship and/or friendship.
- Young adults desire to process hurts or frustrations with others who may have already experienced what they're going through.

- Young adults have an apparent desire for relationships that exemplify learning from others' wisdom and experiences.
- Young adults are in search of mentors that model everyday living.[15]

Young adults need and long for older adults to mentor them. Their hearts' desire is for people of age to journey alongside them. They are simply waiting for the church to create a setting of inter-generational people that feels natural and where authenticity is promoted. They not only want to learn life skills, they also want older adults to unveil their mishaps and struggles and tell them what they've learned in the process. No setting meets these expectations better than a healthy intergenerational small group.

It is in this setting that a healthy exchange of passion and information is passed between the two generations when they have the opportunity to do life together in an intergenerational small group. This is a two-sided coin. Spence Shelton, small-groups pastor at The Summit Church in Durham, North Carolina, put it this way: "In our church, we are seeking to push through consumer-driven community to family-style community. We say around our church all the time that a small group of nineteen-year-old men is much closer to *Lord of the Flies* than it is biblical community! So we encourage our group leaders to seek out some people who are in their life stage, and others who aren't. This isn't just for the sake of the next generation either. Older generations feed off of the energy younger people bring to the community. I've got a guy in my small group who is my dad's age and who has become a close friend of mine. He put this concept best when he said to me, 'Spence, my generation runs the risk of sitting around remembering what God *did*. We are here in your group because we want to believe the best years of following Christ are *ahead* of us. And that is how you "younguns" think.' The older guiding the younger, and the younger emboldening the older."

Fact #5: Not-Yet Adults Add Much to the Small-Group Experience

The age-graded grouping paradigm is deeply ingrained. In fact, thinking of a child or a teen being in a small-group meeting with his or her parents seems . . . well . . . wrong. Our mental image of a group experience doesn't have children in it. But is it possible we are missing out on the power of the Holy Spirit working through children?

Randall Neighbour, a cell-church guru, once reminded me that when children receive Christ, they are not then filled with a miniature Holy Spirit. The same Holy Spirit indwelling every adult in a small group is also supernaturally at work in and through any child and teen who is a follower of Christ. God longs to use them when the group meets.

I was once leading a small group that was not intergenerational. While the adults met, we had child care for the kids in a different room in the home where we met. One evening as we were getting ready to take the Lord's Supper together, a parent asked if we could include the children who had become followers of Christ. I hesitated, but the group pushed me. I didn't want to lose "the moment" with kids being kids. When the children joined us, I asked if someone would pray before we began. One of the kids piped up and said he'd like to. To be honest, I was sure this was going to be a lost moment. But when this nine-year-old prayed, I wept. His sincerity was obvious, his faith was real, his love for Christ portrayed a passion that had been lacking in my life for many years. The Holy Spirit was speaking through this young boy, and we were reaping the benefits of the work of the Holy Spirit through him. It was a glorious, God-honoring, unforgettable moment.

We don't take note of the work of the Holy Spirit in and through children because when they are used by the Spirit, we often diminish what just occurred to the "Wasn't that cute" category. A ten-year-old speaks words of wisdom, and we think or later say, "Wasn't that cute?" A twelve-year-old humbly reminds an absentee mom that her kid needs her. We think or later say, "Wasn't that cute?" A five-year-old prays a prayer full of faith and expectation. We think or later say, "Wasn't that cute?" Because we have responded this way so long, we often don't even realize just how powerfully God can use a child if viewed as an equal in an intergenerational small group.

Randall Neighbour's book *The Naked Truth About Small Group Ministry* relays two stories that shouldn't go unheard:

> A small group was meeting and one member was absent with a migraine headache. The group's leader asked a child to pray for her. The child prayed, "Dear Lord Jesus, please make her better. Take away the pain and don't let her die. Amen." The adults laughed and spent some time reassuring the child that she would not die. The next day, the leader called to see how the woman was feeling and spoke to her husband. "Haven't you heard? She has meningitis. But thank God, she did not die from it." A child does not dwell on logic but moves spontaneously bypassing the logic of man to respond to the heart of God.[16]

Yet another real-life experience reminds us that children sometimes depict the Holy Spirit at work in the face of adversity:

In a restricted access nation, a small group of Christians gathered in a home, knowing the danger it posed for the homeowner and members. The police arrived, spat on the Bible, and demanded each person deny Jesus or be shot in the head. A child stood up and wiped the Bible with her dress saying, 'Jesus, I am wiping the shame off your Word.' With that, she was killed.[17]

I will confess, having children and teens as part of a small group makes it necessary for the adults to sometimes have to get together outside the meeting time to discuss sensitive issues. Children will be a distraction at times and, yes, their parents will have to teach them how to respond to, respect, and do life with adults. But the payoff for everyone involved will be extraordinary.

Fact #6: Intergenerational Grouping Gives One-Parent Kids Two-Parent Relationships

It is no secret that one-parent homes are not only acceptable, they are the norm in today's society. This means that in a one-parent home, one of two households exists: a mom and her kids or a dad and his kids. Any child living in a one-parent home is at a great loss as he or she is without a connection to or a model of either the male parent or the female parent.

While a group member can never replace a mom or dad, they can be the friend and mentor to a child whose home is void of one gender or the other.

I will not soon forget a call I received as I was driving home from work one evening. It was the spouse of one of our church members. On her way home from work herself, she'd just received a call from her daughter who had arrived home to find her dad in bed but not moving. This was a bad situation and I knew it.

I was at least thirty minutes from these precious people. I called her small-group leader. He didn't hesitate to go to that home. He was there with this wonderful woman and her children when I arrived, grieving with them. These kids had lost their dad and a vibrant woman her husband. A few months later the daughter's school scheduled a "dad day." Obviously, this was going to be a tough time for this young girl. It would have been even more difficult but for this one fact: She had a surrogate dad. One of the men in the group agreed to go to school that day and act as a stand-in dad.

This young lady had lost her dad but she was not and still today is not lacking someone who loves her like a dad and is going to be the model of a Christian husband for her.

One of my closest friends is Dave Hall. Dave is an ex-athlete standing 6 feet 4 inches tall. He's a man's man with a desire to mentor teenage guys. Dave has chosen to own and oversee his own small farm, partially so that he will have a place and way to speak wisdom into these future leaders. Many a young man has spent hours upon hours working alongside Dave. While they are together, Dave is not only teaching them how to drive a tractor, hammer a nail, and dig a posthole, he is also instilling his Dave-isms in them. I can't imagine that there's even one of those young men who doesn't cherish the relationship and sometimes longs again for Dave's wise counsel.

Boys need men in their lives. They need godly men to teach them how to do certain things. They need to see how they treat their wives and how they relate to other men. They need to know how to respond when you lose your temper or lose a friend. They need a model so that they too can someday be godly men and husbands. An intergenerational group creates a scenario that makes it possible for a boy without a dad to have a surrogate father who can instill many important skills and understandings and model being a godly man.

Fact #7: Intergenerational Grouping Gives Older Adults a Chance to Pass On Their Wisdom to the Next Generation

It is in living life that we learn life. And those who have lived it the longest are often full of wise counsel. The question is, What is the most natural and effective setting to receive wise counsel from those who have lived more life than we have? There is no better setting than in an intergenerational small group.

In a small group, couples unveil their marital struggles and individuals make known their inner turmoil. In a small group, we are apt to discuss the right thing to do in the most difficult of situations. In a small group, parents ask for wise counsel concerning parental issues. In a small group, people ask those of age about the stage of life they are experiencing and how to cope or grow during this life stage.

Intergenerational grouping gives older adults a chance to pass on their wisdom to the next generation, and most are longing to do just that.

Let's face it: There are at least seven good reasons to consider intergenerational small groups. Perhaps some of these reasons will resonate with you. We need to remember more than anything else that intergenerational small groups obviously have a place in our world and the time God dropped us in. Considering intergenerational groups may be the start of an amazing journey for the people who are your church.

CHAPTER 5

THE FOUR QUADRANTS OF GROUP LIFE

THE QUADRANTS

Some of the primary goals of a tribal CMC are the elevation of Jesus; transformation of individual hearts; having a personal, local, and global missional mindset; and a common community working in tandem with the Holy Spirit to create an environment where these expectations are experienced. This environment is created when a CMC is involved in four expressions, the four quadrants of group life: theological, familial, restorational, and missional.

Theological

I am using the term *theological*, but it is important that we embrace theology that is correct, not perverted. Let me explain. Most sincere followers of Christ would agree with the principle behind the theological term "the sufficiency of Scripture": "The idea that Scripture contained all the words of God he intended his people to have at each stage of redemptive history, and that it now contains all the words of God we need for salvation, for trusting him perfectly, and for obeying him perfectly."[1] Scripture rightly interpreted gives us all the information we need. The problem is that interpretation has sometimes been replaced with opinion, opinion that starts with Scripture but ultimately ends in perversions of truth.

CMC leaders must be aware of three perverters.

1. Mistaken Voices of Authority

Biblical interpretation definitely has its perverters, and many of them have been given the authority and title by a denomination, seminary, or church to declare to others what the Bible says. Because these people have the title of bishop, seminary president, seminary professor, or pastor, people in a CMC quickly accept their interpretation as truth. After all, they are well-studied theologians dishing out theology, so the average believer eats up and digests that theological perspective. Why? Because people much smarter than they, whose office walls hold evidence of multiple seminary degrees, individuals who have been empowered by an organization the average Joe believes in to divvy out biblical understanding, have espoused what is believed to be correct theology. The masses in their organizational circle have embraced it, so it gains a blind hearing.

Right or wrong, entire denominations, nondenominational churches, house churches, and small groups buy in to someone's theology because they believe the leader has based his or her perspective completely on Scripture. But sometimes that theological bent is not founded on Scripture. If the truth were known, sometimes this person's perspective is based on what is acceptable to the masses. In this situation, culture trumps truth, and a new and perverted theological perspective is now firmly in place.

Please don't misunderstand: I'm talking about only a minute number of thinkers in the roles mentioned. But in an era when celebrity pastors are unwilling to say whether or not the only way to God is through Jesus Christ and when entire denominations are welcoming church leaders into high levels of leadership whose lifestyles are undeniably sinful, we have to take note. There are some mistaken voices of authority.

Some theologians pervert truth, but they are not the only contaminators. Secondary ideologies are also pollutants. Some eras in Christian history seem to embrace and integrate a secondary ideology or theory into the interpretation of God's Word. When this happens, we begin to interpret what God is telling us through two lenses rather than the only authoritative lens, God's words revealed in the Bible. These lenses differ from era to era. Let me speak of the two I've seen in my lifetime.

2. Psychology over Theology

For decades, theology has been invaded by psychology. Now don't get me wrong—psychology is very important to emotional health. It is vital in evaluating where God needs to be at work in someone's life and often plays an important role in the healing process. But when a group tries to conclude what God is telling them and psychology is the channel to His perspective, a theological perversion will often be the outcome. Have you been in a Bible study when the group was seeking to realize what God is saying and someone announced, "Dr. Phil said on his show a few weeks ago . . ." or "My counselor has told me over and over again . . ."? Some will quote the latest self-help book written by a celebrity psychologist or psychiatrist as if to say, "We now know what this passage means because someone who really understands the human condition has given us understanding."

When something of this nature occurs, Scripture is no longer the bottom line. Dr. Phil or a group member's counselor or the author of the latest "how to make yourself whole" book is. And in many instances, if the truth were known, many in the group are more apt to embrace the ideology of the psychologist than biblical theology.

Culture has taught us to do this. Biblical theologians are no longer known as those who have the answers to life's questions; psychologists and psychiatrists are. Watch any newscast or talk show. If the host wants an expert opinion concerning how to live life or how to be whole, a pastor isn't the one seated in the guest seat, it's a well-known expert who has training in psychology.

Culture gave psychology top billing, and in some settings the church subconsciously welcomed it as the new and foremost ideology.

3. Philosophy Above Theology

For the last ten or so years, philosophy has invaded theology. When discussing Scripture, anyone's philosophy gets thrown into the conversation. Four philosophical voices often seem to trump the pure words of God:

- The voice of philosophical heroes, people like Gandhi and Oprah.
- The voice of the community and individuals a group member spends most of his or her time with. Some, maybe all, of them declare their own brand of belief, and

because of one's relationship with them or respect for them and because it sounds so right, the group member accepts the idea being espoused.

- Every individual's personal truth. We live in a society in which the term *my truth* has become a cliché, as much a part of the common conversation as any. Only 9 percent of people who call themselves born again believe absolute moral truth exists.[2] Every individual's perspective concerning truth is as good as any.

- Yourself. Because we live in a generation of people slow to read, study, and memorize God's Word, some perspective comes to mind and because we don't have a firm biblical foundation to stand on, our perspective "feels right," so we inadvertently accept it as factual.

When authoritative voices misinterpret, a psychological or philosophical perspective is given precedence over truth, or we accept anyone's idea of truth as truth, confusion holds a CMC captive and keeps them from experiencing healing, transformation, and an unfathomable experience with God.

These perverters could be termed "impersonators." They are not the real thing, yet many have embraced them because they look and feel like the real thing. We live in an era when impersonators of each of the quadrants have, in the minds of many, replaced the pure principles that are vividly disclosed in Scripture. The theological replacements are psychology and philosophy. I want to be very, very clear — psychology and philosophy are important to the world and should even speak into the journey of every believer. Only when a small group allows their ideologies and theories to trump biblical truth should there be concern.

A group that functions mostly in the theological quadrant makes its primary objective to study the Bible.

Familial

The term most often used to describe relationships between small-group members is *friends.* In fact, many pastors tell those who are new to their church that they'll "make friends" if they join a small group. But God wanted so much more for us when He adopted each of us and connected us to a Christian community. He wanted us to realize that we are part of a family, brothers and sisters doing life together until we are taken by the Son to be with God our Father.

Spence Shelton, the small-groups pastor at The Summit Church in Durham, North Carolina, put it this way:

> When the Bible talks about the church, it uses the metaphor of a family. When Christ is asked about his family who is waiting outside for him in Matthew 12, he refers to his followers as his family. Jesus was redistricting the family by a new blood line . . . his. The church, those claiming the blood of Christ, are now to function as a family. Paul jumps on this referring to his readers as brothers and sisters throughout his letters. Like any family, this family would have older members whose responsibility would be to raise up younger members (Titus 2). It would be a community where you lived alongside one another in the rhythms of everyday life (Acts 2). God's design for the church was not just new spiritual friendships, the church was to be a family.

Joseph H. Hellerman nailed it when he wrote *When the Church Was a Family.* This astounding book unearths the metaphor of family that Jesus used when He spoke of the church. Hellerman wrote,

> The closest same-generation family relationship was not the one between husband and wife. It was the bond between siblings. The particular characteristic of the Mediterranean family should markedly inform our understanding of Christian community, since the idea that we are brothers and sisters in Christ constitutes the fundamental conceptual point of departure for coming to grips with God's social vision for his church. No image for the church occurs more often in the New Testament than the metaphor of family, and no image offers as much promise as "family" for recapturing the relational integrity of first-century Christianity for our churches today.[3]

Changing the paradigm of our group members' relationships with one another from friendship to family is vital and difficult. It is vital because healthy family units made up of mature brothers and sisters:

- Will not bail on one another when conflict occurs
- Cannot overlook a brother or sister's emotional or financial needs
- Instinctively nurture and protect the less mature sibling
- Are willing and available to give wise counsel and hold siblings accountable if their actions or activities are damaging them
- Celebrate one another's wins and grieve each other's losses
- Realize that their role and goal is to please their Father and so they all live under His directives, which ultimately strengthens and unifies the family

It is vital for a small group to view one another as family.

And it is difficult because of the era in which we are leading groups. It is difficult to change the paradigm of your group from friends to family because the image of family hosted in the hearts of many has a very negative connotation. A significant percentage of the population comes from homes of divorced parents who engaged in an ongoing battle for the love of their children, and many others have been raised in homes of dysfunction. While many can embrace the culture's description of what a family is, we cannot overlook the void and inner struggle that is created when a child grows up in a dysfunctional home or the home of an angry and bitter single parent. Neither can we look aside when Mom and Dad are vying for time with their child. We have to notice the relational longing that is experienced in the human heart when separated from siblings or when children are devastated by being brought up in an environment void of consistency, traditions, and healthy oneness.

All of us long for a healthy family and memories of one. When thinking of the family unit in which we were raised, each of us should feel warmth, have fond memories, and be reminded of the most secure relationships anyone will ever experience. But for many, when reminded of biological family, there is only a cold world void of consistency and security.

These negatives open the door wide for God's family to fill the void created by unhealthy biological families. Everyone longs for a family that gives him love and security, hope and help, and the freedom to be himself without being judged or ridiculed, a group of people who establish family-like rituals and relationships and care for one another deeply enough to live life for the betterment of each other.

John Burke said,

> God had a plan to create a new family, a redemptive family — a
> family with the power to heal and restore what humanity lost by
> going its own way. Ephesians chapter three says this is a mystery
> of God, that through Christ we can reconnect to the Father as a
> new family. A family that "being rooted and established in love,
> may have the power, together with all [God's people], to grasp
> how wide and long and high and deep is the love of Christ."[4]

The goal of every CMC should be to become a family, not
best friends or close confidants; the goal shouldn't even be to
become a healthy small group. The goal should be to become a
family guided by the expectations of the Father, held hostage by
the hope we all experience in Jesus, and to become a spiritual
household. A group that functions mostly in the familial quadrant
makes its primary priority to do life together in biblical Christian
community.

Familial relationships have their own impersonator: disposable connections. There is a great difference between a familial
relationship and a disposable connection. As mentioned earlier,
family members cannot easily bail on one another as they are
tied together forever because they are blood relatives, they
are forever family even if the relationship is strained. This was
God's intent for believers, that they be forever family, bonded
together in a forgiving, caring, and unending relationship for all
of eternity.

But, even in church life, we find an impersonator that is
wreaking havoc on the body of Christ, making connections
disposable. If someone has a beef with another person, in many

instances, instead of working to heal the wounds, walking away from the relationship has become the norm. For a small group to become all it was meant to be, there will be conflict. In years past, many embraced the biblical expectation to make amends, not make for the exit door. But today many are willing to simply throw the relationship away and find a new crowd to hang with. From the very beginning of the group's life together, relationships are perceived as disposable, a connection that can easily be disconnected if all doesn't go as anticipated.

Restorational

Jesus disclosed His love for humankind and His longing to be a restorational Savior when He announced,

> The Spirit of the Lord is upon me,
>> because he has anointed me
>> to proclaim good news to the poor.
> He has sent me to proclaim liberty to the captives
>> and recovering of sight to the blind,
>> to set at liberty those who are oppressed,
> to proclaim the year of the Lord's favor. (Luke 4:18-19)

Jesus is the restorational expert, and He gave every small group all the tools it needs to work with Him to see those in emotional captivity set free. He frees those who are blind to the effects of sin but are trapped in it. He sets "at liberty those who are oppressed" by the outcomes of their own debilitating choices or the choices of those who played significant roles in their story.

The restorational quadrant comes to play in every healthy tribal group. You'll see it anytime that:

- A relationship (marriage or friendship) is in jeopardy
- An addiction is revealed
- Someone unearths a devastating past experience or ongoing traumatic situation that has created emotional trauma such as physical, emotional, or spiritual abuse
- A group member is forced to deal with a devastating loss such as the death of a family member, the exit of an adult child from the home, or the loss of a job
- A past sin is being used by the Enemy to hold a group member in an abyss of shame and guilt
- A group member is experiencing debilitating depression

A tribal small group is vividly aware that we live in an era of unbridled sin, confusion, and mistaken choices. Some, maybe many, individuals in CMCs need the restorational power of Christ to be received in Christian community. Jesus paid the ultimate price on the cross so that all could know what it means to live a life free of guilt and shame and wake up every day knowing they have been liberated.

Restorational groups fall into two categories: healing groups and support groups. Healing groups want to see group members set free from the hurts of the past that have created emotional baggage and, perhaps, addictions in the present. They also aim to bring healing to relationships that need to be mended. Support groups are created to support members through natural life stages or life situations that are unchangeable. These include experiences such as grieving the death of a friend or family member, the exit of the last child to leave the home (the empty-nest syndrome), the loss of a job or joblessness, a group of people gathering because they all have a child who is autistic, and many more.

Impersonators of restoration include actions taken to "medicate the pain." Because the church lost her faith in Christ to heal the brokenhearted and to set free those in emotional bondage, she is forced to consider how to diminish the pain of those who are hurting. The answer is to help people find ways to medicate the pain. This could be through pills or meeting with a counselor whose goal is to relieve some of the emotional pressure at each session.

Please know that I am not suggesting that using medication when necessary is a bad or wrong choice. For those with a life-long chemical imbalance, medication may be God's gift to bring balance and emotional consistency to their lives. And for many who are struggling with depression and other short-term debilitating emotional difficulties, medication is often necessary as these individuals are in process and moving toward emotional healing.

Missional

Every small group and every member of every CMC was rebirthed to missional living. Ed Stezer, vice president of research at LifeWay Christian Resources and the author of *Planting Missional Churches* and *Breaking the Missional Code*, described being missional this way: "I think simply at its core, missional means to join God on mission because He is the source of that mission, the center of the church. I tend to define that as meaning that the church would act in missionary ways, would design and focus itself around the mission of God."

Being on mission is not the same thing as being missional. My friend Scott Boren reminded us:

Helping the lost or the poor, while good, is not what I mean by being missional. Service projects are good; feeding the poor, packing lunches for the homeless, and sharing your faith are noble tasks. But God's missional rhythms run much deeper than a list of tasks in a culture that plays the rhythms of the FedEx life. We must learn to be relational in the way we interact with one another and in our neighborhoods. Too easily we turn being missional into a project in which those of us inside the church perform some action for those outside our church.[5]

Individuals that make up a missional small group are careful to notice the needs of group members as well as the needs of those outside the group. They see their part of the world, whether that be where they work, where they live, where they vacation, or the ball field where their child plays soccer as a place where missional opportunities may arise. They see the world through missional lenses, and when there is a need to be met, a word of encouragement to be voiced, or an opportunity to tell someone spiritually dead how Christ can bring him or her to new life, missional people respond accordingly.

Missional group members are more spontaneous than programmed. Like Christ Himself, as they go about their daily routine, when a need is noticed, they strive to meet that need individually or invite their group to work alongside to meet that need. They are not waiting for the church to plan a mission trip, organize a work day, or hand them tracts to quote to neighbors who are blindsided by their unscheduled knock at the door. While these individuals are willing to be and effectively are on mission when the church calls, they are more apt to see an opportunity and seize the moment than wait for an organized effort to be planned for them.

And a missional CMC does more than just meet needs. To simply meet needs leaves the story only halfway told. A missional

CMC is made up of people who realize that the meeting of needs gains them the credibility to share the gospel with those whose needs they are meeting. While the motivation for meeting the need is not necessarily for the purpose of sharing the gospel, they are praying for and anticipating God will make that possible.

When missional small-group members speak of the gospel, it is not a foreign object they stumble over. They speak of Christ, their journey with Him, and the transformation they have experienced that is made possible for all as naturally as they speak of the relationship they have with their closest friend or spouse.

Tribal small groups understand the importance of being missional together. They embrace the fact that those far from Christ see Christ when a small group works to be Christ to the neighborhood where that group meets. They see the location where they meet as a mission house for the people on that street or cul-de-sac. They are the missionaries to the subdivision or in the community where their group gathers. Eugene Peterson interpreted John 1:14 this way:

> The Word became flesh and blood,
>   and moved into the neighborhood.
> We saw the glory with our own eyes,
>   the one-of-a-kind glory,
>   like Father, like Son,
> Generous inside and out,
>   true from start to finish. (MSG)

A group's most potent entryway into the hearts of those who are not yet followers of Christ is not in the knocking on doors and quoting some predetermined salvation sales pitch. It is in a small group being the church by doing good deeds. In so doing, a group opens the door to verbalizing the gospel. But being missional together does so much more for a group than making it possible to unveil the gospel.

I will never forget the day our small group entered a home in Spring Hill, Tennessee. One of our small-group members knew of the need and facilitated our spending a Saturday helping a struggling family. This was a desperate situation, one that actually created a bit of uneasiness in some of us. The household was a one-parent home and two people in that house had been diagnosed with and were being treated for cancer. When we entered the home, we were quickly aware that either this was a scene from the TV show *Hoarders* or this poor mother, in caring for her children, didn't have the time to organize and clean house. We quickly learned the latter was most likely the reality.

The group had been assigned tasks. Most were immediately put on cleanup duty. The leader of this project decided that we were going to organize and clean this woman's house before the day ended. I went to work installing grab bars that would make it easier and safer for someone with a physical disability to get in and out of the bathtub. Other duties were assigned and everyone went diligently to work. This was a monumental task. It wasn't a job anyone would have chosen to do. After all, how many people want to give up another Saturday and how many people, if they have a Saturday available, want to clean their own home let alone someone else's? But it was an important day for our group.

Being missional together has many amazing and important outcomes for a small group: (1) It bonds a small group as nothing else will. Anytime a small group works together, laughs together, and experiences accomplishment together, a bonding takes place that is very special. And when a group is working together, laughing together, and experiencing this in the midst of meeting someone else's need, the bonding is exponentially magnified. (2) It aids a group in seeing the neighborhood and community through watchful eyes. As a small group begins to realize the importance of and opportunity in doing good works, they will begin to be more attentive. They'll notice a broken window in a single mom's home, a widow's lawn that has gone unmowed, a household that seems to be struggling to make ends meet, and more. (3) It helps group members realize and exercise their spiritual gifts and abilities. And (4) it allows a small-group leader to see who in the group has leadership potential.

A missional small group is a humble and powerful force, a quadrant of small-group life that transforms not only those who are on the receiving end of the group but also the giving end.

Even missional living has its impersonator: needs meeting. Meeting needs definitely has its place, but when a CMC allows needs meeting to replace missional living, it takes Jesus and the gospel out of the equation. Let's face it:

Needs Meeting + No Story = Needs Met
BUT
Needs Meeting + Jesus' Story = Abundant and Eternal Life with Christ

Jesus is the centerpiece of missional living. We meet needs because of Him, and when the Holy Spirit makes a way, we speak of Him because of the love He has shown to each of us and because we know what He is willing to do for those whose needs we are meeting.

THE SYNERGY OF THE FOUR QUADRANTS

Tribal CMCs are engaged in all four quadrants, but they are not trying to balance the amount of time spent in each quadrant, nor are they being careful to give equal energy to each quadrant. There are many reasons why a group cannot give equal time to all four quadrants: (1) the primary passion of the small-group leader, (2) the curriculum the group is using, and (3) the needs of the group members.

All small-group leaders have a quadrant they are most passionate about. This may be due to the spiritual gifts they've been given or the enthusiasm they have for a people group. For instance, a small-group leader with the spiritual gift of teaching will most likely lead his or her CMC to giving more time and attention to people learning God's Word, the theological quadrant. This is what is natural and normal for a leader with the gift of teaching. A leader who is passionate about those who are struggling financially and/or without a relationship with Christ will most likely drive his group to be mostly missional. When a leader has experienced and overcome substance abuse or has been on the verge of divorce but God restored his heart and/or healed his relationship, this leader is apt to lead the group to be mostly restorational. And a small-group leader who is longing for and in need of substantial connections with other believers will be most focused on familial living; her group will give most of her attention to the familial quadrant.

Curriculum choice may determine which quadrant of group life is primary to the group. For instance, if a CMC is using a Bible study that has daily homework, Scripture memory expectations weekly, and in-depth teaching on a specific book of the Bible, this group is going to be a theological group. But if the group is using a curriculum that is guiding members through the process of emotional healing due to a past experience or an addiction like alcoholism, pornography, or overeating, it is a restorational group.

The needs of the members may determine which quadrant a group gives most of its attention to. Let's say a group leader has a group of married young adults all of whom work full-time jobs and have preschoolers at home. The most important need of this group may simply be to spend time with those who are on the same journey. They need a family to talk to, brothers' and sisters' shoulders to cry on, and one night a week when they can let their hair down and enjoy the company of other believers. This group is going to be more of a familial group.

But don't be confused. Every group is involved in all four quadrants.

As you look at the following diagrams, you'll be able to see the four group types and how they look when in action.

Diagram 1

Diagram 1 shows what a theological group looks like. As you can see, the largest piece of the pie is the theological piece. This piece is the reason the members chose this group. They want to study the Bible. The group leader chose to lead this group because Scripture is his passion and he longs for others to grasp its truths as much as he does. But notice, the other three quadrants are still part of group life. They are just smaller pieces of the pie. The CMC has as its focus being theological but it is still familial, restorational, and missional.

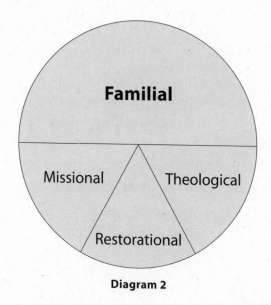

Diagram 2

Diagram 2 depicts a familial group. The largest piece of the pie is familial. But the group doesn't ignore the other pieces of the pie; they are less but they are not overlooked. The group is also diving into Scripture, meeting needs and unearthing the gospel to those far from Christ, and restoring one another's hearts as the group lives in Christian community together.

Diagram 3

Diagram 3 illustrates a restorational group. This group is formed around the need to overcome an addiction, heal a broken relationship, or gain support through a difficult time. Even the restorational group continues to engage in God's Word, being missional together, and functioning as a family unit.

Diagram 4

Diagram 4 portrays a missional group drawn together by a passion to be missional together. While they are about missional living, they are still studying the Bible together, functioning as a family, and restoring one another's relationships and broken spirits as the need arises.

As you can see, each group type has as its primary goal to give major attention to one quadrant of group life while engaging in the others secondarily.

CHOOSING THE RIGHT PRIMARY QUADRANT

Choosing the right primary quadrant for a small group is one of the most vital decisions a CMC leader will make. If the wrong quadrant is chosen, the group leader may not lead with a contagious passion. And a leader lacking in passion will in time create a passionless group.

Three questions must be considered when determining which quadrant will be a small group's primary quadrant.

1. Is there a primary quadrant the church is requesting a group make its quadrant of greatest focus? There are times when a church's leadership asks a group to assume a particular primary quadrant. It could be as the small-group ministry is being started or when a group system is geographically based and a particular group type is needed in a specific region. It could be that the church leadership is in the process of making sure many types of groups are available and they need a particular type of group to fill gaps. Whatever the reason, the church leadership may expect a group leader to lead a specific type of group.

2. Which quadrant is the small-group leader most passionate about? The most effective leaders will lead a group whose primary quadrant is in sync with their primary passion. In most instances, if the small-group leader has the gift of teaching, he or she will be most excited about leading a group whose primary quadrant is theological. If the small-group leader longs to see believers live in unity and experience the beauty and power of pure Christian community, the group should make its primary quadrant familial. If the small-group leader has experienced broken relationships, overcome addiction, or has a passion to lead people toward the redeeming power of Christ, that individual would be most effective leading a group whose primary quadrant is restorational. If the small-group leader has the gift of apostleship, evangelism, or mercy, he or she will do best leading a group whose primary quadrant is missional.

3. Which quadrant would be most important for the betterment of the group members? Some CMC leaders take the pulse of their group members and, before determining which quadrant will be the primary quadrant, conclude which of the four quadrants is most important to their group at this point in their journey. For instance, if the group is made up of people who don't know how to pray, the group leader will make the group's primary quadrant theological so members can focus on learning a biblical perspective on prayer. If the group is made up of people most of whom are dealing with loss, the group should become a group with restorational as its primary quadrant. Bottom line, the small-group leader wisely concludes where the group members are and responds by choosing the group quadrant that takes them further along in their journey or establishes spiritual practices leading to ongoing growth.

QUADRANT SHIFTING

While a group may be primarily theological, familial, restorational, or missional, it needs to be willing to shift its primary quadrant for a time if necessary.

Quadrant shifting needs to take place when: (1) the Holy Spirit does something that demands it, (2) a group leader realizes there is a knowledge void or a skill needs to be known or learned, (3) the need of a group member or the group becomes known, or (4) several people in the group are in a new season of life.

The Holy Spirit will sometimes direct a group to move from one primary quadrant to another for a period of time. Let's imagine the Holy Spirit speaks to the group leader or a group member who is part of a familial group. The Holy Spirit anticipates the group will set aside its regular agenda and take some time to care for a family in which the dad/father is soon to die of cancer. This group will shift from being a familial group to being a missional group until it is free to revert to being familial. For a visual of this, looking back at the diagrams just viewed, the group will shift from being a diagram 2 group to a diagram 4 group and will, at some time, return to being a diagram 2 familial group.

Sometimes a group leader discovers a knowledge void or a skill that the group members need to know or learn. This is especially true if the small-group leader is leading a group of young believers. Let's say the leader of a missional group notices that these passionate group members don't know how to share the gospel with someone. The group may need to shift for a period of time to being a theological group so that the members can study and learn how to teach someone how to become a follower of Christ. For a visual of this quadrant shift, look again at the diagrams. In this situation a group will, for a time, shift from being a diagram 4 group to being a diagram 1 group.

Sometimes a group must shift from its primary quadrant to another quadrant because a group member's need is unearthed. For instance, if a couple in a familial group announces to the group that they are on the verge of divorce and they are crying out to the group to help them, this CMC may need to shift to being a restorational group for a period of time to work with the desperate couple so that their marriage can be restored. In this situation, a diagram 2 group shifts to being a diagram 3 group throughout the process.

And a group will need to shift to another primary quadrant if several or most of the group members are heading into or find themselves in a new or challenging life stage. Let's say several couples meeting as a theological group, find themselves overwhelmed by the fact that most or all of them are empty nesters and are dealing with the emotions that accompany this new stage of life. This group may need to shift from being a theological group and give their hearts to supporting one another by becoming a restorational group. This would mean the group moves from being a diagram 1 group to functioning as a diagram 3 group as the group members transition into the empty-nest reality together.

A group leader may ask, "What do I tell the group when we make this shift?" There are two ways to handle this. The first would be to show the group the diagrams that you have just been looking at and get the group's permission to make the shift. A second option would be to say nothing but to make the shift.

As you can see, the group will still be involved in the quadrant that has been life to the group; it will just be a smaller piece of the pie. In most cases, group members will not even notice that the shift has taken place.

Be careful though. If a group exits its primary quadrant for too long, group members may feel duped if they joined the group because of its (previous) primary objective/quadrant. If the shift is noticed and lasts too long, group members may bail.

GUIDING A GROUP TO BE THE FOUR QUADRANTS

One of the most important shifts we have to make in the tribal small-group world is the shift from telling group members "what to do" so that they meet the local church's requirements or so that they will help the church to grow larger, to helping group members understand "who they are to become" and helping them become that as they join the movement to grow the kingdom of God.

A tribal small group has as one of its goals to help group members become theological, familial, restorational, and missional people. Many churches—due to their need to meet budget, have enough workers to service the church's many programs, and make sure enough church members are going on mission trips—have their own quadrants, and those quadrants most often reflect "doing" more than "becoming." A church might have as its quadrants: Link (join a Sunday school class or small group), Give (tithe), Assist (take on a responsibility in one of the many ministries of the church), Go (go on a mission trip or help pay for someone who is going on a mission trip). Each of these has as its primary objective to let church members know what the church expects of them. Church members are told how they can help the institution, which is not welcoming to the new generation of churched individuals.

The new responsibility of the small-group leader is to help each member not only know and be involved in the four quadrants of group life but also "become" each of the quadrants individually and to live them out in community. A small-group leader can consistently do some specific things that will further this goal:

- *Espouse each of the quadrants.* When a well-established influential leader advocates the four quadrants, followers who believe in the leader also believe what he or she advocates. A leader who has fully adopted and embraced each of these four quadrants will greatly influence group members if he speaks of them often and is a consistent proponent of them.

- *Be verbally repetitive.* Repetition is the key to terms becoming internal realities. A small-group leader needs to speak often of them, especially when the terms are new to the group. At every gathering, tie them to group life. Each time the group is going to be on mission, speak of being "missional." When the group starts the Bible study time, remind the group that they are going to be "theological." Use the term *restorational* when a group member has unveiled a need to overcome an addiction or a relationship needs mending. And when talking about how the group is to relate to one another, be bold enough to voice the term *familial.*

- *Be the model.* People do what they see done. When a small-group leader models "four-quadrant behavior," others will follow his lead. The small-group leader can be a model by reminding the group during Bible study time that the group is striving to be "theological," then recounting living missionally by helping out a homeless person, taking a meal to a lonely neighbor, sharing the gospel with someone at work, or any other missional activity. By doing this, he or she models and helps establish what it means to be a "four-quadrant group member."

- *Affirm group members at every opportunity.* Affirmation establishes what a group leader really wants members to be about, builds up the group member being affirmed, and leads to that member acting in the same way in the future. When a group member tells you he has lived life in one of the quadrants, privately affirm him. Verbalize how proud you are of him and how grateful you are that he too is joining you on the journey.

- *Create heroes.* Everyone wants to be a hero for others, and when a small-group leader creates heroes, everyone else realizes what is really being asked of them. When a small-group member acts in one of the four quadrants, a small-group leader can establish him as the momentary hero by telling the rest of the group what he has done or by allowing him to tell his story. It would even be wise to start the story by saying "John is my hero," followed by the story being told. But it's not only in doing that heroes are created. Sometimes a hero needs to be created when someone simply embraces a quadrant he or she has been struggling to accept. For instance, if a group

member has been questioning the responsibility to be
missional at work or on the street or cul-de-sac where he
lives, if he tells the group leader that he has embraced
the responsibility of the biblical idea of being missional,
this heroic acceptance opens the door to tell that person's
story.

- *Connect the four quadrants to biblical conversations.* Each
time a small group meets, the most important story of
all, the Bible, is revealed and discussed. Many of the
stories and most of the principles unearthed in Scripture
make it possible to tie one or more of the quadrants to
individual lives and group life. For instance, as David
meets Goliath, all four quadrants are at play. Group
members could easily find themselves discussing a theological perspective as they become immersed in principles that can flow from this historical account. A familial
conversation may ensue as the group considers the way
David was treated by his brothers, opening the door
to discuss how we are to treat our brothers and sisters
in Christ. A restorational conversation may come into
play as the group discusses how God might go about
restoring a Christian community (whether that be a
small group, a local church, a denomination, or the body
of Christ worldwide) that has fearfully allowed pagan
religions to invade its space. And a missional conversation could come about as the group realizes that there
is a people group at war with God's people, people who
need to know David's God.

   When a small-group leader brings to the forefront
or ties any or all of the four quadrants to individual life

situations or communal life together, the small-group member's heart begins to connect and embrace the quadrants and the power each of those quadrants can have as they continue on his spiritual journey.

- *Compose communal agreements.* The terminology used in the past for a list of agreements has been *covenant.* Over the years the term has picked up serious baggage. For many, it's become synonymous with demands and unfair expectations. In the post-Christian era, I believe using the term *agreement* is much more welcoming and effective than the term *covenant.* In order for a communal agreement to lead toward being more than doing, we must reconsider what these agreements look like. On page 114, you'll find a communal agreement that may be workable for your small-group ministry.

You may have noticed that as often as possible, the title of each of the categories speaks of Jesus. If the makeup of a group represents today's culture, and if the group is reaching out to those far from Christ or cynical about the church, Jesus is the one factor that resonates with all. Even the most fanatical atheist believes Jesus was a good and caring person. Those who disdain the church have a high regard for Jesus. No matter what someone's belief or lack of belief, the historical Jesus rises above all hesitations. His lifestyle, His caring heart, His passion for the down and out, His compassion for all, cannot help but be revered by everyone in the group. Allowing Christ to be the centerpiece of group life, no matter who is in the group, will make it possible for all to gain entrance into the conversation and ultimately into unity of spirit and purpose.

Communal Agreement

In order to be a healthy group, I will:

1. Keep everything discussed between group members confidential
2. Attend every group meeting unless there is a major situation that keeps me from being at the group meeting
3. Do all in my power to forgive any person with whom conflict arises and will strive to resolve any conflict in a timely fashion
4. Welcome each person's opinion and be respectful of him or her even when we disagree
5. Do all in my power to protect the hearts of my fellow group members

In order to become more like Jesus, I will:

1. Study Jesus' story as seen throughout the Bible, and allow it to shape my actions and attitudes
2. Engage in discussions with the group without dominating the discussions
3. Be willing to accept direction from my fellow group members when appropriate

In order to experience the inner peace Jesus offers, I will:

1. Be willing to journey into my own story
2. Be willing to allow Jesus' story to speak into my story
3. Be willing to do this because the other group members allow me to do this at my own pace

In order to show the heart of Jesus to the world, I will:

1. Take part in the missional experiences of the group when possible
2. Do all in my power to meet the needs of my fellow group members
3. Strive to allow myself to begin to see the world through missional lenses and respond accordingly
4. Work with our group in the starting of another group

With Jesus as the starting point, those who are not His followers when the group starts will realize over time that the primary personality in the group is Jesus. This will allow the believers in the group to speak of Him and make the not-yet followers of Christ aware of His work in their lives. The gospel will be revealed and will transform lives.

CHAPTER 6

THE MAKEUP OF A TRIBAL SMALL GROUP

"**A** tribe is a group of people connected to one another, connected to a leader, and connected to an idea."[1] Seth Godin didn't realize it when he penned these words, but he landed firmly on the definition of a tribal CMC. A tribal CMC is most certainly a tribe. We are connected to one another because we are friends. We are connected to a leader, the leader of the group. And we are connected to an idea—the life, attitudes, and activity of Jesus. You may be asking yourself, "Why didn't Howerton say, 'We are connected to one another because we are family'? 'We are connected to a leader, Jesus Christ'? and 'We are connected to an idea, the gospel'?"

I didn't describe a tribal CMC in this way because everyone in the group doesn't consider himself part of the Christian tribe. As mentioned in the introduction to this book, a tribal small group, due to the era in which we are living, will include people from various ideological perspectives. They are not yet part of the church, do not believe that their leader is Jesus Christ, and are not yet gospel-centered people. Every *believer* in the group needs to be made aware that he is the church, that his leader is ultimately Jesus Christ, and that the gospel is what connects him to the other believers in the group.

The makeup of a tribal small group takes on a flavor different from what we may have embraced in the past. Because there are many ideologies, much brokenness because of past hurts and dysfunctional relationships, and because the group is journeying into synergies not realized in groups past, it will be made up of an array of people.

SYMBOLIC ROLES

When we acknowledge the following types of people and make it possible for them to be who they are, the timbre and dynamic of the group will change immensely and lives will be changed as never before.

Convinced Biblically Functioning Followers of Christ—While no one will arrive at complete spiritual maturity this side of heaven, there are those in small groups who are fully convinced, biblically functioning followers of Christ. With all of their being, these people are striving to live lives as outlined in Scripture.

Saved Cynics—No follower of Christ aims to be cynical, but most believers are spiritually cynical at some time in their lives. This is because a current life situation is overwhelming or because a situation is out of one's control. And some are cynical because they have been spiritually abused. At some point in their journey, these people felt they were mistreated by other followers of Christ or a church leader. They often distrust other believers, even their small-group leader. They will sometimes allow sarcasm to be the mode through which they reveal their cynicism. Still others who are saved cynics are cynical because Christians in their past mistreated them. The more intimate the broken relationship, the more cynical the person will be. If a supposedly Christian mom, dad, grandparent, or best friend mistreated the person by being unwilling to offer forgiveness, blatantly and purposefully contradicting biblical expectations after being a model or mentor, or turning his or her back on God and in so doing retreated from a relationship with the cynical group member, a cynical heart may result.

Secularized Strugglers — Secularized strugglers may or may not be followers of Christ. They are group members who tilt more toward secular ideology than biblical theology. Secularized strugglers who are already followers of Christ have allowed and may still be allowing secular perspectives to be their true north. Scripture is important to them, but down deep in their hearts, their worldview is anything but biblical.

Not-Yet Converted Conversationalists — Not-yet converted conversationalists are, in most instances, my favorite people. They are people who are exploring spirituality or Christianity. They are willing to join in the dialogue concerning Christ and Christianity, but they haven't yet crossed the line of faith and become followers of Christ. They add much to the conversation and force all group members to know what they believe and why they believe it.

FUNCTIONAL ROLES

Leader — Every movement of any size must have leadership, whether we're talking about a CMC or the Reformation. And a healthy CMC will experience the kind of intensity and momentum that accompanies a movement. My definition of a leader is someone with "the ability to obtain and retain followers, organizing them, unifying them, and directing them to accomplish a God-given vision." The leader of a tribal small group obtains followers by asking others to join him on the journey, retains followers by having a lifestyle much like that of Jesus, organizes followers by giftedness and the ability to do the work necessary for the group to thrive, and unifies them by asking all to make communal agreements and hold to those firmly. The leader directs the group by proactively leading members to the next step of group life as the group does life together.

Leader in Training—Healthy small groups multiply, and every new group needs a leader. In order for a small group to birth a new group, a trained leader must be available. The best way to create a new leader is to have a leader in process walking alongside and learning from the present leader. This is the leader in training.

Missional Coordinator—In order for a group to effectively and consistently be involved in mission together, it is important that it have someone who is responsible to keep missional efforts in the forefront of the group, responsible for seeking out missional opportunities, and coordinating the ministry to be accomplished.

Host—The host is responsible for making sure the meeting location is known by all, coordinating food, and creating an environment where everyone feels welcome and at ease. This role is especially important in a tribal small group. If a group is to represent the culture, there will soon be members from all socioeconomic situations, all ethnic groups, and various belief systems. Coming to a home where many of those in the room are carrying Bibles, praying to the Christian God, and discussing life from a mostly Christian perspective will be very intimidating to many who are joining the group. The host is vital as he or she will create an inviting environment and through conversation help those who are not yet at ease to begin to feel at home.

Child-Care Coordinator — If a group does not choose to be intergenerational in nature, it will need someone responsible for child care. This person is the child-care coordinator.

You may have noticed that I didn't include two roles that have been the norm in many past group-life systems: (1) fellowship coordinator and (2) care coordinator. This is strategic and purposeful. Here's the deal: One of the primary values that is intuitive in a tribal group is authenticity. When something that should come naturally is programmed — that is, institutionalized — it is no longer perceived as acted on simply because group members love one another and care for one another as a healthy family would. If a group has to appoint a fellowship coordinator so that members relate to one another outside of group meetings or a care coordinator has to be put in place so that needs are met, members will quickly sense they have become part of an organization rather than a loving, caring community.

SHARED ROLES

Spiritual Parents (Almost Everyone) — Spiritual parents are those who realize and embrace that they are part of a spiritual family and that they have journeyed places others have not yet gone or are spiritually more mature than someone else in the group. Spiritual parents accept their role and administer parental care, give wise counsel, and protect those younger in the faith. In a tribal small group, almost everyone is a spiritual parent as almost everyone is further along in the journey than someone else.

Fellow Journeyers or Spiritual Children (Every Believer) — Being spiritual children is a mindset each group member must embrace. In the tribal small group, each member acknowledges that he or she is a child of God the Father, under His direction, and learning to serve Him as a fully devoted follower of Christ. Each person also realizes and accepts that some in the group are more spiritually mature or have lived more life — spiritual parents who help nurture spiritual children.

Spiritually Gifted Equals (Every Believer) — A thriving small group in the tribal world will quickly acknowledge spiritual gifts, help group members find their gifts, and not only allow group members to use their gifts but lead them to use their gifts in group life. It is vital in the tribal small group that the leader as well as anyone with any gift recognize that all gifts are equal. We must remember that any elitism in a world plagued with church leaders and parents who have created debilitating perspectives of those in authority will be viewed with disdain and hinder the leader's ability to lead. Equality is simply a right perspective and one that needs to be made known and lived out as the group does life together.

THE UNSEEN GROUP MEMBERS

Let's face it — early in a group's life, great small-group leaders look around the room, take stock of each individual, and then determine what gifts and abilities each of these persons brings to the group. That small-group leader then uses those gifts and abilities to create a transformational group. Seldom do we ever consider that there are three invisible members in the group who not only bring their abilities to the group but also are the reason the group exists. They are God the Father, Jesus the Son, and the Holy Spirit.

Does this surprise you? While it is hard to imagine, the fact is that all three persons of the Trinity are with us each time the group is together. For decades, the small-group world has talked about and promoted friendship and relationships between group members. We have spoken of how the circle of friends that make up the small group can become a vibrant community meeting one another's needs. We've promoted holding one another accountable, crying on each other's shoulders, and helping carry each other's loads when the load was too heavy to carry alone. We humans are what make this group a group, and we are what makes this group transformational. Our mental image of a small group includes the faces of those in the circle. But do we need to broaden our view so that we can envision and call on the unseen members of the group?

We have a problem perceiving the presence of the unseen because of our focus on the material. T. W. Hunt put it this way in his amazing book *Seeing the Unseen*:

> Because of our material upbringing, it doesn't make sense to "look to" that which is invisible. That's why to focus on it requires a different kind of attention. To focus on the unseen requires being aware that the unseen is the always-present background of something other than what we can touch or manipulate. It means considering the unseen in every decision and act.[2]

Imagine how fantastic a small group will be if it would simply "look to that which is invisible" and consider "the unseen in every decision and act." CMCs miss out on much because they focus only on the faces that are seen while inadvertently ignoring the all-powerful abilities of the Personalities that are unseen.

When **God the Father** is given His place in the circle, selfless attitudes are intuitive, a transformational environment is created, and every person in the room is forced to consider both his sin and his future service. We see this as Isaiah found himself in the presence of God. Check it out:

In the year that King Uzziah died I saw the Lord sitting upon a throne, high and lifted up; and the train of his robe filled the temple. Above him stood the seraphim. Each had six wings: with two he covered his face, and with two he covered his feet, and with two he flew. And one called to another and said:

> "Holy, holy, holy is the LORD of hosts;
> the whole earth is full of his glory!"

And the foundations of the thresholds shook at the voice of him who called, and the house was filled with smoke. And I said: "Woe is me! For I am lost; for I am a man of unclean lips, and I dwell in the midst of a people of unclean lips; for my eyes have seen the King, the LORD of hosts!"

Then one of the seraphim flew to me, having in his hand a burning coal that he had taken with tongs from the altar. And he touched my mouth and said: "Behold, this has touched your lips; your guilt is taken away, and your sin atoned for."

And I heard the voice of the Lord saying, "Whom shall I send, and who will go for us?" Then I said, "Here am I! Send me." (Isaiah 6:1-8)

- Humility is a natural outcome as group members realize how small and insignificant they really are as they intuitively compare themselves to the almighty God (verse 5). Healthy humility creates an attitude of equality between group members, making it possible to share openly and in all humility speak into each other's worlds.
- An awe-inspiring fear of God and His words creates healthy boundaries for the group's conversation, allowing it to make substantial headway in seeking God's

perspective concerning His Word instead of allowing
personal opinion, past experience, or ideas and ideologies
accepted by our culture to drive the conversation
(verse 4).

- The sin in each group member's life becomes evident to
him or her as no one can be in the presence of a perfect,
sinless, holy God and be unaware of personal shortcom-
ings (verse 5).

- Individuals allow God to reach out and cleanse them
of all of their sin. In so doing, they experience the inner
peace that accompanies clean hands and a pure heart
(verse 7).

- Every person is reminded that he or she is to leave the
group experience to be on mission (verse 8).

When **Jesus the Son** is given His place in the circle of
relationship, group members are continually reminded that they
are able to be in the presence of God and that they have a priest
who is continually interceding on their behalf.

Hebrews 10:19-22 reads,

> Therefore, brothers, since we have confidence to enter the holy
> places by the blood of Jesus, by the new and living way that he
> opened for us through the curtain, that is, through his flesh, and
> since we have a great priest over the house of God, let us draw
> near with a true heart in full assurance of faith, with our hearts
> sprinkled clean from an evil conscience and our bodies washed
> with pure water.

Old Testament priests entered the presence of God from time
to time on behalf of the people. Only the high priest could enter

the Holy of Holies, the place where God's presence dwelled. But when the perfect high priest, Jesus, was crucified, offering Himself as a perfect sacrifice, the curtain that closed off the Holy of Holies was torn in two from top to bottom. This unparalleled moment in history indicated symbolically that access to God in heaven was open to all of God's people from that point on. Jesus made a way for any person in any and every CMC to have access to God so that he or she can constantly "draw near" to God with "full assurance" and without fear. Realizing that Jesus is with us is a constant reminder that God is with us and we with Him.

And when group members acknowledge that Jesus is with them, they are also vividly aware that Jesus, God's Son, is interceding for them to the Father. Another priestly function in the Old Testament was to pray for the people. Jesus, the Great High Priest, is interceding before God at all times. Both the writer of Hebrews and Paul, the author of Romans, confirmed this:

> Consequently, he is able to save to the uttermost those who draw near to God through him, since he always lives to make intercession for them. (Hebrews 7:25)

> Who is to condemn? Christ Jesus is the one who died—more than that, who was raised—who is at the right hand of God, who indeed is interceding for us. (Romans 8:34)

When a small group seeks the healing of a sick body or a broken heart or is asking for forgiveness to be given and received—or perhaps for someone to begin a friendship with Jesus—Jesus isn't going to appear before God with broad-stroke requests. Jesus is so in tune with our emotions and our passions that He is going before

God on our behalf with very specific requests. When unpacking these two passages of Scripture, Wayne Grudem wrote,

> The word *intercede* translates the Greek term *entygchano*. This word does not mean merely "to stand as someone's representative before another person," but clearly has the sense of making specific requests or petitions before someone. For example, Festus uses this word to say to King Agrippa, "You see this man about whom the whole Jewish people petitioned me" (Acts 25:24). Paul also uses it of Elijah when he "pleads with God against Israel" (Rom. 11:2). In both cases the requests are very specific, not just general representations. We may conclude, then, that both Paul and the author of Hebrews are saying that Jesus continually lives in the presence of God to make specific requests and to bring specific petitions before God on our behalf.[3]

And when the **Holy Spirit** is acknowledged as a present personality in the group, He will guide, teach, and unify the group.

Throughout Scripture, the Holy Spirit guides people's paths. It was the Holy Spirit who led Jesus into the wilderness after His baptism (see Matthew 4:1). It was the Holy Spirit who told Philip to walk alongside the chariot carrying the Ethiopian eunuch until Philip was invited to explain what the Ethiopian was reading from the book of Isaiah (see Acts 8:29). It was the Holy Spirit who told Peter to go with the three men who came to him asking him to go to the home of Cornelius (see Acts 10:19-20).

And the Holy Spirit is the one who teaches certain things and makes it possible for group members to understand what is being taught. Jesus told His disciples that the Holy Spirit "will teach you all things and bring to your remembrance all that I have said to you" (John 14:26). Jesus also announced to His disciples, "When the Spirit of truth comes, he will guide you into all the truth" (John 16:13).

The indwelling Holy Spirit is also at work in every CMC creating supernatural unity. Following Pentecost, the Holy Spirit fashioned a new kind of community—the church. The believers were marked by unparalleled unity. Paul described it like this:

> And all who believed were together and had all things in common. And they were selling their possessions and belongings and distributing the proceeds to all, as any had need. And day by day, attending the temple together and breaking bread in their homes, they received their food with glad and generous hearts, praising God and having favor with all the people. And the Lord added to their number day by day those who were being saved. (Acts 2:44-47)

This unity was not produced because the people were living in community; it was because the Holy Spirit had created in each person a longing to be community for one another.

As a CMC meets, it is wise to remember that the unseen members of the group are there, intermingling with the group, interceding for the group, and making it possible to experience unfathomable unity in the group.

GATHERING A TRIBAL SMALL GROUP

Discerning who will join a leader in a tribal CMC is the first question a leader asks. In many churches this question is easily answered. Perhaps there has been a campaign to get church attendees to sign up for a small group — announcements made by the senior pastor during weekend worship services, e-mails sent out, blog posts produced, tweets tweeted, professionally produced posters lining the walls of the church — all in hopes of seeing a vast number of people go online and sign up for a group or show up at a designated location in the church lobby to register. If this isn't a church's practice, maybe it uses a connect event. In this situation, those who want to be part of a group show up for a few hours, and they are given some instruction, taken through a creative experience, and placed in a group before they leave the room. These are all very impressive and effective ways to get church attendees to join a group. If they're the outgoing type, the knowledgeable crowd, the relationally adept group, they long to fall in line with the church leadership's expectations and have a belief system that is, for the most part, in line with the ideology the church espouses. These people are the "easy to assimilate into church life" audience.

Let's push the pause button for a moment and clarify some-thing about small-group ministry. In many churches, the church leadership aims primarily to assimilate people into church life. Assimilation means getting those who have attended weekend worship involved in all of church life. In these churches, the leadership often has a clear path for anyone who has attended the church a few times or is interested in becoming a "church member." The prospects will attend a "Get Acquainted with the Church" class before they are considered members of the church. While in the class, a person is asked to choose the ministry area he or she is willing to serve in, connect with a small group, and in some cases agree to tithe and attend weekend worship services consistently. Studies have shown that if a person is involved in a small group, attends weekend worship services, is giving finan-cially to the church, and is serving in a ministry area, he or she is most likely going to stick (that is, not only be on the church's roll but also be involved in the church's ministries for years to come). This is a common practice. Assimilation has been accomplished. The outcomes are obvious—the church roll has added more people, there's a crowd in the worship center during weekend worship services, and these individuals are on various ministry teams helping the church to function efficiently and effectively. This is a very successful way to not only involve those believers who are totally on board with church life but also to see a church running on all pistons.

In a church longing to assimilate well, those who have attended weekend worship services are the ones most likely to fill small groups because service attendees have heard about or have been invited to join a small group. And those who have heard the pleas or attended the connect event are most likely those who are outgoing, biblically knowledgeable (those lacking biblical knowledge are often intimidated by small groups), relationally adept, quick to follow the requests of the church leadership, and who share common beliefs. These are the types most likely to sign up for a group.

I hope you captured the last few sentences of that paragraph. Do you see the insinuation? Those who are outgoing will be looking for relationship, so they are most likely the ones who will seek out a group experience. Those who are biblically knowledgeable are on board because they feel at ease when discussing the Bible and may even find a piece of their identity in their knowledge of it. Those who are relationally competent feel comfortable with other people. They know they won't "blow it" relationally, so they will likely consider a CMC. The people who always follow those who lead have a penchant for joining a small group as they submit to authority in almost every setting and probably have most of their lives. And those whose belief system is foundationally the same as what they are hearing in sermons are likely to sign up for a group.

But what about those who are not amateur Bible scholars, those who consider themselves relationally incompetent, those who are not submissive to authority, and those whose foundational belief systems may not even come close to paralleling the church's? What about them?

We must keep in mind that due to the influences of today's culture:

1. Many people are not face-to-face conversationalists. They lack experience with eye-to-eye relationships because of the ease and acceptable practices of online conversations, texting, and e-mails.
2. Biblical illiteracy is an epidemic.

3. Norms no longer specify how people should relate to one another. Because of this, many have acted in a way that seemed right and acceptable, but the outcome was disastrous. They have become relationally gun-shy and may be hesitant to join a small group.

4. Authority figures are suspect, so many people are unwilling to blindly do what church leadership requests.

Due to biblical illiteracy in a culture that welcomes anyone's truth as correct and in a world where tolerance trumps questioning even ridiculous theories, many are hesitant to join a group as they don't want to create tension or meet people trying to convince them that they are wrong or that their family members or friends have been or are being deceived.

We must remember that countless people never make it into a CMC. Many of them are Christ followers who love the church but aren't comfortable joining a group. Many of them are pre-Christians, willing to converse about spirituality. But these believers and unbelievers are often overlooked. As a small-group pastor evaluates the percentage of weekend worship attendees in groups, he or she may rationalize that the percentage of weekend worshippers in groups is the norm while overlooking these two groups of people that could benefit greatly from a small group. Please allow me to be very blunt. If you're a small-group pastor, accepting the norm can mean tens, hundreds, or thousands of people in your church are not going to connect with a group where they can hear and process the gospel. Or, believers will not grow in their relationship with Christ through the synergy of Christian community. In such cases, accepting the norm is unfathomable.

We need to begin thinking differently, and we may need to consider some fresh ways to gather CMCs.

WHO SHOULD BE INVITED INTO A TRIBAL CHRISTIAN MICRO-COMMUNITY?

Anyone with a brain, a heart, and a pulse is the answer to this question. And the more diverse the group, the healthier it may be. For generations the church has grouped already-churchgoers together via life stage or age. There is certainly nothing wrong with this, and CMCs can be grouped by life stage or age. But tribal small groups are asking different questions now. In the past we've asked,

- "How can we get more people into groups?" In making the numbers of people in groups the marker by which we judge our small-group ministry's effectiveness, is it possible we've overlooked the process through which transformation takes place?

- "What should our groups study or do during their group meeting that is enthralling enough and comfortable enough that they'll come back to the group every week?" Is it possible that by making the goal consistent attendance, we've downgraded what happens when a CMC gets together, and as a result, something substantial seldom occurs?

- "What expectations should we have of group members so that they'll continue with the group?" Is it possible in so doing we've slowly evolved into a ministry that expects less in people's lives than Christ requests of every one of His followers?

Also, a CMC doesn't ask, "Who thinks like me?" but rather "Who thinks?" When a tribal small group gets together, we hope that people from various belief systems are in the group.

It may start with six prayerful Christ followers. Over time those disciples may attract people in a broad array of ideologies. Perhaps the group will someday include not only six believers but also people journeying spiritually who are currently into agnosticism, Buddhism, humanism, or witchcraft. Let's face it—if we're going to reach people in many settings, especially urban settings, this may be the makeup of our neighbors and coworkers. Anyone who is willing to hear the gospel can be influenced by it.

A tribal CMC doesn't ask, "Who lives like me?" It asks, "Who lives?" Someone once told me she wanted to be placed in a group with people of the same socioeconomic status. She wanted to be certain she could attend theatrical productions together and shop with the people in her group. These were her recreational activities, and they were high on her priority list. She needed to be sure everyone in her group could afford to enjoy the things she already was enjoying. Socioeconomic status has no place in a tribal small group. If a person is alive and is capable of connecting with a small group, no matter what his social standing or income, he is welcome.

A tribal CMC doesn't ask, "Who looks like me?" A tribal small group asks, "Who looks?" Diversity of age and ethnicity is a great gift to everyone in the group. We learn from one another's experiences and stories. Those who have known what it's like to have lived through a world war, to be African-American living in the South, to be from South America working as a chef at a local restaurant, to be homeless, or to be a college-educated person of European descent will all gain from the experiences and perspectives of one another. Tribal small-group members are blind to age, ethnicity, and social standing and are welcoming of anyone—as Christ was.

A tribal CMC doesn't ask, "How is this going to enhance my life?" A tribal CMC asks, "Whose life can I enhance?" Many times people in groups are looking out for their own interests. If the truth were known, they are considering a group or are part of a group because of what it does for them. Tribal small-group members focus on giving back to others rather than seeking their own interests. They are not looking for people to become part of their group because those individuals will enhance their lives; they are looking for people to join their group whose lives they can enhance.

So who should be invited into a tribal CMC? Anyone. And where do I find these people? Everywhere. They live in the houses on your street or cul-de-sac. They reside in the apartment building where you live. They work in your office building. They exercise at your gym. They are the parents of the kids on your son's soccer team. They are the single mom or single dad of the kids standing next to you as you wait in line to pick your child up at school. They shop where you shop. Every person you come in contact with is a potential tribal small-group member.

RECRUITING PEOPLE INTO CMC LIFE

Most growing churches know how to make church members aware of small groups. They publicize them through worship guides, newsletters, and announcements at weekend worship services. These are all important and effective ways to make the church aware of small-group opportunities. However, I believe we should reconsider the language used when promoting groups.

Language Matters

The motivators for becoming a group member must change — that is, if we're going to see those on the outskirts of church life committing to the inner circle of group life.

In the past, the small-group world has used some of the following phrases to draw people into group life:

1. Make friends.
2. Learn and grow in the knowledge of God's Word.
3. Be held accountable.
4. Meet one another's needs.
5. Become a mature disciple.

Some of the new motivators and language might be:

1. Go on a spiritual journey with fellow journeyers.
2. Explore the answers to life's complex questions.
3. Be yourself while becoming something more.
4. Never go it alone.
5. Make a difference in the world in which we live.

The new reasons for joining a small group not only parallel those in the first list, they also use language that is acceptable, maybe even motivational, to the saved cynic and the secularized struggler.

The new reasons for joining a small group parallel the first list:

1. "Make friends" and "Go on a spiritual journey with fellow journeyers" are alike in that they have the same goal in mind. But using the terms *spiritual journey* and *fellow journeyers* shows that the goal is so much more than making friends. The primary goal is to realize and explore spirituality together, and in the process substantial relationships will happen. Because the group is made up mostly of Jesus followers, it will be evident to everyone

that the Bible will be the foundational ideology. But, because of the use of the term *journey*, those who are not yet followers of Christ or who are cynics instinctively believe — and rightly so — that the group is open to allowing the conversation to take many and varying ideological paths.

2. "Learn and grow in the knowledge of God's Word" and "Explore the answers to life's complex questions" are one and the same yet different. When someone hears or reads the first phrase "Learn and grow in the knowledge of God's Word," his first thought is that he's going to be involved in a Bible study, that the group will open up the Bible and someone will read it and declare to everyone what it says. This in and of itself may keep many in today's diverse ideological world from considering a CMC. When we use the phrase "Exploring the answers to life's complex questions," there is a perception that (1) the group is going to seek answers to the questions that people are really asking and (2) the group will be made up of others in need of the answers to life's questions, which equals conversing for the betterment of every person in the group.

3. "Be held accountable" and "Be yourself while becoming something more" are a walk down the same path, but the second option is much more palatable in today's world and removes the legalistic terminology. The term *accountable* insinuates to those who misunderstand Christian accountability a checklist created by the institution so that everyone falls in line with the institution's preset code. It declares that you're not good enough so we'll keep you in check. The second phrase, "Be yourself

while becoming something more," welcomes each person
as acceptable right where he is while making sure each
person knows he is going to continue to become more
than he is at present.

4. "Meet one another's needs" and "Never go it alone" are
somewhat alike. "Never go it alone" is stronger because
so many have known abandonment. Mom or Dad
walked out on the family, friends bailed because there was
conflict, siblings wrote them off because of the dysfunction that existed in the home of their upbringing. The
inner turmoil and the voices inside of these people declare
over and over again, "You are alone," "You are alone,"
"You are alone." Belonging to a family has become more
important than ever because when someone is truly part
of a family, he never feels he will have to go it alone.
Not only that, when we say "Meet one another's needs,"
many who are lacking in resources may determine that
they are unable to help in the meeting of someone else's
needs, that there is an expectation of all group members
that they cannot meet, which will ultimately cause them
embarrassment and may keep them from getting involved
in a CMC.

5. "Become a mature disciple" and "Make a difference in the
world in which we live" are parallel in this way: Each of
these phrases implies that the world, present and future,
is being affected by group members' actions. But in a
world in which people are motivated by reaching out to
those who are less fortunate locally or on the other side
of the globe, the imagery of affecting the world has a
greater draw than becoming a mature disciple. Not only
that, for those who are already followers of Christ, they

may envision hours of daily homework, fasting, and changing everything about their present lifestyle in order to become a mature disciple, something they are not yet ready for.

The tribal CMC must remember that its primary reason for existing is not to get people to commit to church life. Remember what was stated on page 130: "Studies have shown that if a person is involved in a small group, attends weekend worship services, is giving financially to the church, and is serving in a ministry area, he or she is most likely going to stick." If the institution and its leaders are suspect and those who are furthest from Christ are the ones most suspect of them, when recruiting group members we must stay away from promoting the sponsor church. *Please don't stop reading now!*

I am not suggesting that the local church isn't critical — she is the bride of Christ. Nor am I insinuating that the group should hide who it is from those it is inviting into a CMC. What I am stating is that, if we're going to reach those far from Christ who are disappointed with, angry with, or disgusted with the local church, the best recruitment tool isn't an announcement that the local church is the reason the group exists.

We have to ask a couple of probing questions:

- Is it more important that the person journey toward Christ or journey into church attendance?
- Is it possible the person will become part of the church after he or she becomes a follower of Christ?

The answer to each of these questions is obvious. It is most important that those who are not yet followers of Christ journey into a relationship with Him and, if they follow the normal pattern, end up as part of a local body of believers.

Obviously, some will come to the weekend worship services and find Christ there. But more and more, the local church has baggage that many not-yet followers of Christ are not going to give the necessary energy to unpack. They are going to listen to the gospel because someone builds a relationship with them, connects them to their friends who are believers, and invites them to join these new friends in group life at the God-appointed time.

INFLUENCING THOSE FAR FROM CHRIST INTO A CMC

When inviting a person far from Christ to consider joining the group:

- Build a friendship with him or her. This could take days, weeks, months, even years. During this time, speak of your group just as you would talk about anything else you are involved in and passionate about. Talk about the group just as you would golfing, shopping, camping, or any other thing in your life you really enjoy. A strong caution—build a friendship but do not consider this individual a project. Too many followers of Christ aim to "make someone else a Christian." First off, you can't prompt someone else to become a follower of Christ; that's the work of the Holy Spirit. Second, if you have the "this person is my project" mindset, you'll bail on the relationship when you grow tired and think that you're not going to accomplish your ultimate goal, to make a Christian out of the person. At this point, you make an enemy and you diminish the influence all other followers of Christ might have in that person's life in the future.

- Invite your friend to hang out with the CMC when the CMC is involved in something recreational away from the group meeting time. Friends introduce friends to friends. This is just the way we do life. It would not be unusual for anyone to invite someone they've become friends with to hang out with and get to know their other friends. This is normal and natural. When your small group is getting together for dinner, a movie, or a cookout, invite your new friend to the outing or gathering. Connect your friend to your friends in your small group. Continue to do this until the unbeliever is just another friend that everyone enjoys hanging out with.

- When the individual you've befriended asks about the group, tell him or her. It is at this point that you have to be very sensitive to the Holy Spirit. Your friend may be asking questions simply because he or she wants to understand what a small group does or is or has as its goals. There may be no inclination on your friend's part to join the group. Listen to the Holy Spirit, and if prompted, invite your friend to the group.

- Continue to enjoy the friendship and continue to invite the person to group experiences until he or she seriously considers being part of the group or joins the CMC.

This progression is natural, authentic, time and personality sensitive, and void of sterile invitations and slick marketing. Some will say that it's too time consuming, too slow to connect individuals to "Bible study," or lacks a call to follow Christ quickly enough.

Here's the deal: In today's world, we gain a hearing by being a trusted friend. And becoming a "trusted" friend takes time, energy, and stick-to-itiveness. It demands meeting one another, both parties concluding they'd like to get together again, finding common ground, exploring over time if the acquaintance may become a friendship, establishing that the two parties are friends, which opens the door to hear and explore one another's stories, sticking around even after revealing each other's stories, being there for one another when life is perplexing, then continuing on a relational journey together. And this could take months or years.

CHAPTER 8

THE TRIBAL CHRISTIAN MICRO-COMMUNITY GATHERING

CHANGE THE TERMINOLOGY FROM *MEETING* TO *GATHERING*

Let's revisit the term we've used to describe a group's getting together. For decades, a small-group rendezvous has been termed a *meeting*. But we should reconsider this term for several reasons:

- For those whose life has been or is business, politics, or community advisory boards, the term *meeting* carries with it reminders of fighting for one's idea or perspective and making decisions based on opinions rather than coming to determinations based on God's perspective. While it may be subconscious, clinging to the term *meeting* may be very detrimental. The very attitudes and environment created in most meetings is diametrically opposed to what we are trying to accomplish in a tribal CMC.
- The term *meeting* has the scent of "institution" all over it. It describes making decisions or having discussions that

will benefit those higher on the organizational flowchart.
Many will hesitate to join a group if they see the group's
primary purpose is to serve the institution. While wise
group leaders need always keep in mind that they are
accountable to those in leadership, they are also aware
their group may function within the boundaries set by the
leadership while letting members be the primary decision
makers for their group.

- The term *gathering* simply means that the group is
  together. Their getting together means they may be
  doing anything as long as they are together. In decades
  past, the group meeting was a night set aside for food,
  prayer, and a conversational Bible study. This implied
  that the only really substantial experience included these
  three expressions. The implication was that a group
  gathering to meet the needs of someone newly widowed
  or getting together to have a cookout while inviting
  families with no form of faith or going to someone's
  home to pray for a sick child was less significant. The
  group meeting and those actions associated with it was
  the epicenter of group life, and everything else paled
  in comparison. But a tribal small group realizes and
  accepts the fact that what Jesus said is true: "Where
  two or three are gathered in my name, there am I among
  them" (Matthew 18:20, emphasis added). And wherever
  Jesus is, in whatever setting the group is in, something
  amazing can happen.

   A healthy group realizes that sometimes the most
important thing it can do to strengthen the group is
gather for some other purpose than to have a Bible study.
A healthy group takes into account that the Holy Spirit

may make members aware of a need, so they choose to be missional the night the group normally meets. A healthy group realizes that healthy marriages are vital to the kingdom so they may cancel their normal meeting night, use the already scheduled child care, and do a group date night together. And the list of options could go on and on. Please know that I'm not suggesting that any CMC ignore, even explore, stepping away from a weekly gathering focused on prayer and God's Word. In fact, the next section of this chapter outlines a tribal group experience that includes both of these essentials.

I realize that you may be thinking, *Howerton is splitting hairs to microscopic proportions with this deal about what a group experience is called.* But if we're going to move people into new mindsets, we must first remove terminologies that imply nothing has changed.

TEN VITAL AWARENESSES

When a tribal CMC gets together, it's important that we remember that it is made up of saved cynics, secularized strugglers, not-yet-converted conversationalists, and convinced biblically functioning followers of Christ. Most group leaders in decades past have led their group gatherings as though everyone in the room fit in the last category, convinced biblically functioning followers of Christ. Don't get me wrong—it wasn't that we didn't make room for those believers who were ignorant of biblical truth, those whose stories created tension and a slowness to accept the truths unearthed in Scripture, or those far from Christ. In fact, we longed for them to join us and journey with us. We just didn't keep their perspectives and needs in mind when the group was meeting.

If a CMC leader will keep the following ten principles and directives in mind, he or she will be far down the road to connecting with all group members.

1. All of us have fallen or will fall into every one of these categories at some time in our lives. Because of this, we can relate to each other and encourage one another and should find ourselves intuitively empathizing with one another through past discoveries, through influential voices from the past, and through various life situations that have driven most of us into these confusing places. If someone has never acknowledged that he has fallen into the category of saved cynic or secularized struggler, he either has not been willing to listen to his own heart or he has not yet had a life situation in which God didn't respond in a way that seemed right and that would have relieved his hurt and anguish.

2. Tribal group members may have a Mark 9:24 perspective of Scripture. Because they've been inundated their entire lives with educators, media, and other organizations questioning, downplaying, and degrading Christianity and the Bible, group members may struggle with believing truth at first hearing. They have an "I believe; help my unbelief!" mindset as they study the Bible. Most of these individuals don't want this internal conflict. In fact, given the option, they'd immediately accept and take to heart God's perspective, but their minds have been so saturated with question marks that exclamation marks just aren't natural.

3. Tribal group members will "investigate then embrace" the truth rather than "embrace then investigate" it. Because our culture has driven many to go on a Mark 9:24 journey, some group members will need time to hear the truth, question its accuracy, wrestle with its implications, then embrace it. Let's imagine a small group is discussing Philippians 4:19, which says, "My God will supply every need of yours according to his riches in glory in Christ Jesus." The passage is read, and some in the group are celebrating God and His meeting their needs throughout their lives. The group leader notices that one of the group members is struggling with this concept. Through silence, body language, and a quick glance and eye roll, the leader is vividly aware that this group member deeply doubts this truth.

The group leader directs a question at her: "What are you thinking right now?" Her response is telling: "I really doubt that this is so. My brother has worked hard his whole life. He's tried to be a godly guy. At one point he even attended church and was real involved. About two years ago he lost his job. Now he's homeless. His wife divorced him and he can't pay his child support. I don't think he'll ever be financially stable again. How can we believe this stuff when good people are homeless and doing without?"

This young woman's heart will not let her embrace this truth blindly and without time to process it. She has too many questions, too much baggage, too many sensitivities due to a real-life situation to believe this without first investigating it. This will be true of many group members in a tribal CMC. This investigation can take days, weeks, months, even years. In generations past, those who considered themselves growing disciples would embrace the truth blindly then act out the principle or expectation wholeheartedly. Not so with many today.

4. Tribal group members need to discover truth in community. There are a couple of reasons for this: (1) Most people, even the majority of evangelical church attendees, do not have a biblical worldview. They are seeing and studying Scripture through lenses of ignorance. They need a community to process Scripture with them and help them understand it rightly and in the context of a biblical worldview. (2) Many believe that their own interpretation is as right as anyone else's. Their interpretation is sometimes driven by the need to rationalize their past choices, sins that they struggle with or have decided to stop fighting, or because they have personal friends or family members who are involved in some activity that contradicts Scripture. Their starting point for understanding what God is saying is their personal need to justify themselves or those they love. These group members need a small group to help them realize that, by understanding and welcoming God's perspective, He will redeem their past choices, set them free from the sin that has entangled them, and help them understand how healthy followers of Christ humbly and effectively speak the gospel to friends and family members who are continuing in spiritually devastating lifestyles.

5. Tribal group members are comfortable firmly planted in a Deuteronomy 29:29 mindset. Deuteronomy 29:29 says, "The secret things belong to the LORD our God, but the things that are revealed belong to us and to our children forever, that we may do all the words of this law." A Deuteronomy 29:29 mindset means that when Scripture is gray, believers feel no obligation to make it black and white. God obviously can think in dimensions beyond human comprehension. When mankind begins to believe that they can perceive what God is keeping secret, confusion reigns supreme and debates begin. Those debates can happen at a denominational event, in a local church, or when a small group is gathering. The beauty of our day is that small-group members feel no obligation to land concretely on ideological question marks that God has left hanging. And unlike those in the past, we don't need to worry about the inner tension.

6. Tribal CMC members today are more likely to have emotional trigger points than before. In group life, triggers are those things that evoke a noticeable and, in most instances, unprovoked response. For instance, a group might get into a discussion about drug abuse or someone might ask for prayer for a friend who is struggling with a cocaine addiction. Suddenly, and without warning, during the conversation a group member begins to cry. The group leader asks why this topic triggered this kind of emotion. The tearful group member tells the group that her dad was an addict, and due to his addiction, he was abusive. The trigger was the topic. That topic triggered memories or subconscious reminders that evoked an unstoppable response. The response differs from person to person. If someone else had experienced an abusive parent, his response may have been noticeable anger. In some cases small-group members become numb to it all, and their silence when they are normally talkative may be a marker that their triggers have been pulled as well.

7. Most welcome dialogue but will shut their minds off if the Bible study, by design or not, becomes a monologue. This reality is difficult for those of us with the gift of teaching. We long to "lead a Bible study" rather than "create a transformational dialogue." A transformational dialogue makes room for the Holy Spirit to work. It is a conversation that engages all of the group members. A CMC leader crafts questions that guide every willing member to voice his or her own story as it relates to the Scripture being discussed and makes it possible for the entire group to allow God's Word to speak into members' stories, with the outcome being new attitudes, actions, understandings, and mindsets.

8. Tribal group members are hearing "voices" that are not in the room. During a tribal discussion, group members' minds take them back to the voices of their past. Let's imagine a group is discussing Isaac being tricked by Jacob. Jacob deceives Isaac and his father gives him his brother Esau's blessing, a blessing set aside for the oldest son, a blessing that can be given only one time. As this narrative spins out, many voices may be echoing in the minds of group members. One person may be hearing her mother saying, "You are my beautiful, smart, wonderful daughter. You will always be cherished." Another person may be hearing the voice of a father telling him, "You'll never be worth anything. Your brother's gonna really make something of himself, but you're a lost cause." And another group member may be remembering a conversation he had that day: a boss announcing that if he doesn't step up, he may be without a job.

9. Tribal small-group members will not always accept that the author of the study or the lecturer on the DVD is the final authority. Tribal small-group members are more apt to believe those they can reach out and touch, people who have proved reliable over the long haul, friends who have treated them like caring, nurturing family members. Experts on life are those whose lives group members have been able to see in real time, authentic fellow strugglers who have hang-ups, hurts, and a history they are working through while acknowledging that they are still in process. If lives are to be transformed, a group leader cannot assume that members will embrace what the author of the study or the lecturer on the DVD is saying; they need, through conversation, to confirm what has been taught as the group comes to agreement or the group leader discreetly establishes what is factual.

10. Tribal small-group members need the freedom to discuss other belief systems. The world is full of easily accessible information about atheism, Buddhism, agnosticism, and a plethora of other "isms." And most group members will have friends, family members, or coworkers who are toying with or engaged in some ideology other than Christianity. Thus, people in almost every group will be grappling with what they believe. They may be questioning Christianity, wondering how to discuss Christianity with friends pursuing another perspective, or they may simply be looking for a knowledge base to work from when talking with those questioning their being a follower of Christ.

EIGHT LEADER NECESSITIES

When a tribal CMC gathers, the leader must remember the following facts and lead group members to experience them:

1. Involve the Savior. As mentioned, the often-overlooked personality at the group meeting is Jesus Christ. Be sure to remember His presence, depend on His transforming power, and turn to Him every time a transformational moment is possible. While we can't see Jesus or hear His voice audibly, He is at our gatherings and wants and needs to be the most influential person in the room. The rest of us can give opinion; He gives us truth. The rest of us can talk a group member through a problem; He can fix the problem. The rest of us can pray for healing; He can heal. The rest of us can hold someone accountable for sin; Jesus can free group members from "the sin that so easily entangles" (Hebrews 12:1, NIV). Recognizing and depending on Jesus during group meetings is a very important aspect of group life. The synergy of a small group is not all it could and should be unless we recognize Jesus' influence and allow Him room to do what only He can do. When we do this, He will accomplish things far beyond human comprehension.

Welcoming Jesus to be a group participant isn't difficult:

- *Acknowledge Jesus' presence early in the experience.* Sing to Him. If someone in the group plays the guitar, ask him to bring it and guide the group in singing a few worship songs. Another option is to read a few of the psalms that tell of God's power and presence. An even more potent and personal alternative is to speak to Him in prayer. Say something like, "Jesus, we know You are here; please do what only You can do. We look forward to what You have in store for us."

  If a group chooses to sing worship songs, it will be important that the group leader speak with new group members, especially those who are not followers of Christ, before the meeting begins. They deserve to know that the group will be singing songs they do not know and that almost every person in the group was where they are when they first joined the group. It may be appropriate before singing publicly to announce to the group that the new group members don't know the song so they'll simply be listening to the words while the rest of the group sings. This will alleviate any expectations and set everyone at ease. I suggest that anytime a person is at the group meeting for the first time, the group leader do something other than singing to acknowledge Jesus' presence.

- *If a group member is struggling with a personal issue, stop and talk to Jesus about it by praying.* Speak to Him as though He is in the room. After all, He is.

- *When someone is seeking counsel, first ask, What does Jesus have to say about this?* Then ask group members to share what Jesus has to say about the situation in His Word, the Bible. You may need to give the group time to find this information in the Bible, but it will be worth it. Sometimes a group member will voice his or her own opinion. That opinion may contradict what the Bible says. Remind group members that our goal is "to see what Jesus has to say about that."

- *Listen for Jesus to speak.* While it may make some group members uncomfortable at first, when there is an issue the Bible doesn't speak to, ask group members to go to a place where they can be alone with God. Ask them to listen for Him to give direction. Call the group back together in time. In many instances no one will come back with a word from Him; other times they will. Either way, your group members are reminded that listening to God is an important and normal spiritual discipline.

- *When there is an awkward silence, ask, "What do you think Jesus is thinking right now?"* This may sound strange, but it acknowledges His presence and will reboot the conversation.

- *When a group member needs a miracle, request it.* Asking God to do something huge allows Him to be God and you to prove you and your group believe He is God and that you trust Him to be God. He may not respond immediately. He may not respond the way you would like. But expecting mountains to move is part of the faith journey (see Matthew 17:20). Group members will grow if He responds as requested, and they will grow if His answer to your request is no.

2. Engage the senses. Touching, smelling, tasting, hearing, and seeing are God's gift to humankind, and it is through these senses that group leaders have the most influence. Doubting Thomas questioned the validity of Jesus' resurrection. He stipulated, "Unless I see in his hands the mark of the nails, and place my finger into the mark of the nails, and place my hand into his side, I will never believe" (John 20:25). Thomas knew that in touching the Savior he could be most certain that what he had been told was the reality. Aromas can create a pleasing or disturbing environment. We find in the Old Testament that burnt offerings were often described as a "pleasing aroma to the LORD" (for example, Leviticus 1:9; Numbers 15:3). And it is through taste that Jesus determined we would remember Him as we partake of the Lord's Supper.

Through hearing, we find faith as we hear the words of God and believe: "So faith comes from hearing, and hearing through the word of Christ" (Romans 10:17). Seeing can help us understand a teaching. While Jesus was teaching His followers to set aside worry and live by faith, He most likely pointed to the birds swooping down among those who were with Him and observed, "Look at the birds of the air: they neither sow nor reap nor gather into barns, and yet your heavenly Father feeds them. Are you not of more value than they?" (Matthew 6:26).

3. Implicate all in attendance. Some in every group would rather listen than join in, but they are the ones who need, more than others, to join the conversation. Their silence may flow from a subtle confidence. But in most cases, it reflects the insecurity prompted by previous negative responses or silent disagreement. These silent group members may long to embrace the perceived core beliefs of the rest of the group but believe they are outside the box and are afraid to create ideological tension. They may be struggling with a present life situation or past traumatic experience and are afraid to open up lest they release emotions that they believe will make the group uncomfortable. Or these silent group members may have as their greatest fear that which is true of many, many people: speaking in public. Whatever their situation, they need gentle prompting if they are going to join the conversation.

4. Anticipate "extraordinary moments" and respond responsibly. Sometimes the Holy Spirit throws the door wide open for extraordinary ministry to take place, extraordinary truths to be concreted, extraordinary commitments to be made, and extraordinary healing to take place. You don't want to miss the moment because it may be the moment of ultimate individual transformation and a communal experience that changes the timbre of a CMC for the rest of its journey together. If a group leader anticipates these moments, he or she will not miss the moment and will be more apt to respond accordingly. But the CMC group leader must be praying for them, expecting them, and sensitive to them in order to see these extraordinary moments.

5. Summon spiritual gifts. Every believer journeying with a small group has one or more spiritual gifts. These supernatural abilities were given by the Holy Spirit for use in the context of Christian community. All too often those of us from program-driven churches see spiritual gifts as abilities distributed so that the programs of program-driven church run smoothly. For this reason, the gifts of leadership, administration, and helps get way too much press.

Pastors choose a person with the gift of leadership to oversee a program, a person with the gift of administration to oversee the budget of the ministry as well as organize others to accomplish work, and those with the gift of helps to set up, tear down, and clean up after a meeting, banquet, or picnic. It's important to remember that in the New Testament, the church mostly gathered in homes and spiritual gifts were used in this context. So we shouldn't be surprised to find gifts like mercy, encouragement, giving, intercession, and others. They make more sense when we think of individual needs being met rather than their being used to organize events and programs.

Every small-group leader should help group members realize their spiritual gifts, be certain others in the group are aware of one another's spiritual gifts, and call on group members to use their spiritual gifts to meet the needs of others in the CMC. This will strengthen any group. Even during a group gathering, a group leader may want to purposefully and strategically call on a group member to use his or her gift to enhance the experience or to meet a need. For instance, if someone in the group is asking for prayer, calling on everyone to pray for that group member may be impossible due to time. Asking someone with the gift of intercession will assure a prayer led by one person whose faith will bring great hope to the person requesting prayer. If a group member needs biblical understanding, someone with the gift of teaching may be able to, in the moment, reveal what Scripture says. If someone becomes tearful as she unveils a difficult life situation, a member with the gift of mercy may intuitively want to move from her seat to sit next to the person speaking, empathizing to the point that she, too, is moved to tears. This gift oftentimes makes it possible for a hurting group member to know he or she is heard at a heart level, not just an informational level. When the group leader notices someone with the gift of mercy empathizing to the point of visually expressing the shared emotion with the struggling group member, the leader should feel free to ask the empathizing group member to speak what he or she is feeling. This will greatly encourage the hurting group member.

6. Expect the miraculous. The works of God always accompany biblical community. It may be a husband overcoming the fear of praying aloud. It may be freedom from the bondage of addiction. It may be the redeeming of someone's difficult past. It may be a Buddhist realizing there is only one God and that he can connect with that God through Jesus. It may be the healing of a sick body. But where biblical community exists so do the presence and abilities of God. A tribal small-group leader accepts the fact that God is a member of the group and that, because He is with the group, the miraculous may occur. Instead of wondering if Christ will show up, great small-group leaders realize He is always present and at work, and take note of His willingness to do what only He can do.

7. Listen to the heart. Most group leaders are able and willing to follow the directives of the person who wrote the study they are leading. This is vital. But it is even more important that a group leader be able and willing to listen to and follow his or her heart. It is through the heart that the Holy Spirit will sometimes suggest that a group leader veer from the usual meeting flow and move into a dimension of experience outside the norm. It may be that the group is about to pray but the leader senses it best to leave the house and do a short prayer walk. It could be that, during the Bible study time, the Holy Spirit prompts the leader to simply ask a probing question and allow God to be at work through the rest of the evening. It may be that even before the gathering begins, a group member begins to tell about her childhood and the leader's heart demands the group spend the evening ministering to this person's needs and praying for freedom from the past.

Listening to the heart demands a confident sensitivity as well as a willingness to set aside the comfort of being in control and knowing precisely what is coming next. But in learning to listen to the heart, a group leader will also see the greatest transformation in each group member's life.

8. Love people more than ideology. As said before, a tribal CMC will be made up of a very diverse group of people, many holding to ideologies that contradict those of evangelicalism, maybe even Christianity. A tribal CMC leader must understand that his or her primary role is not to convince these people they are wrong. These kinds of conversations can easily lead to tense conflict that ends in a separation from the group. Loving these people and expressing love through action as they journey is the primary responsibility of the leader. As a leader shows love and respect to these people, they will see the love of Christ in the leader and be willing to hear more about the Christ who is the epicenter of the leader's life.

Bottom line—a tribal CMC gathering needs to feel more like a convening of ideological journeyers whose conversation has the Bible as its starting point than a group of churchgoers getting together for a Bible study. And the flow of the experience must be as natural as possible while engaging the group in not only conversation, but experiences that let attendees' stories be told while integrating Christ's story, the gospel, into their own.

BEFORE THE GROUP ARRIVES

Preparing the room for the gathering is important. Be sure there's ample lighting so everyone can see to read, set the thermostat at sixty-nine degrees so that when the room fills it will be about seventy-one degrees, and put away all pets so those who are fearful of them or allergic to them are at ease. If possible, have cookies or something that emits a wonderful scent. Have music playing that connects with most of the group members. It should be loud enough to be heard and quiet enough that conversations can easily take place. Be sure that seating is set up in such a way that each person can see everyone else's eyes and that no one person is the center of attention. Most importantly, spend meaningful time praying for each person in the group. If you know their stories or life situations, ask God to make it possible for the gospel to invade and affect them.

AS THE GROUP ARRIVES, CREATE AN AUTHENTIC CONVERSATIONAL ENVIRONMENT

One of the most important times in a tribal small-group experience is as group members arrive. The goal is to make sure every person feels welcome and that a conversational environment is created.

In decades past, the small-group meeting was kicked off by icebreaker questions or experiences. The goal was to create a relaxed, conversational environment. Every good small-group resource started with icebreakers. When doing icebreakers, every small-group member was forced to respond to a question that could be answered easily. If everyone engaged in the conversation at the front end of the meeting, everyone was more apt to talk throughout the meeting. Although icebreakers are effective, they have become legendary for feeling corny and contrived. In a tribal small group, the leader will want to do a few things as people arrive to create a conversation and then make sure everyone is engaged in that conversation. This feels much more natural and will replace the feeling of attending a "meeting" with other "group members" with the sense of joining a group of fellow journeyers in a conversation. A few ideas:

- As each person arrives, be certain he or she is met with the following relational actions: a verbal announcement that the leader is glad the person is there, human touch (a handshake, hug, or pat on the back), eye contact, and a welcoming comment (something like, "Hi, Joe, thrilled you could make it tonight," "Hello, Sue, so glad to see you. Hope your week is going well," or "Great to see you, Julie. I've been hearing great things about what's been going on in your world this week"). Here's the deal: The first moments of connection set the tone for each individual. If the leader turns his or her back to the person or ignores him as he enters the room, the individual may feel as though he doesn't matter or that someone else matters more than he does. For those going on an honest, seemingly overwhelming journey, missing this moment could cause them to shut down for the rest of the experience.

- Do something that helps create conversation between group members as they arrive. For example, as people are showing up, fill the room with the sounds of classic rock tunes. Before the leader chooses the music, he or she should take into account the median age of the group members. Just as one would do if he is talking with a friend and a song from their past is playing at Panera Bread or some other restaurant, the group leader can start a conversation by simply saying something like, "I'll never forget the first time I heard that song . . ." and then tell his story. Often others will tell their own story, and if they don't, the leader can ask someone else if that song has any memories for him or her.

Another idea is to begin talking about a sporting event that resonates with most. In almost every instance, most of the members will engage in the conversation, especially if they're men. Keep in mind, these things are happening as group members arrive and before calling the group together to start the formal meeting. Remember, the goal is to engage every member in the conversation and for everyone to know he has been heard and blessed when he spoke.

- As the group leader calls the group together and as members begin to sit down together, keep that conversation going for a few minutes. Be sure to ask those who weren't involved in the conversation or those who listened in but didn't say anything what they think about the topic being discussed. If they say they have no interest in it, ask what's been happening in their world that was exciting for them since the group last met.

If your group first gathers around a table for a meal, simply keep the conversation going as you sit down to eat together. Nothing is as good a conversation starter as a meal when everyone is engaged in the conversation and those who are hesitant are drawn into the conversation by a leader sensitive to those who aren't as verbal as others in social settings.

The goal is for every person to speak, for every person to feel heard, for every person to become more confident that he is important to this circle of conversation, so that every person will engage in the conversation throughout the gathering.

THE FLOW OF THE BIBLE-STUDY EXPERIENCE: OUR STORY, HIS STORY, THE JOURNEY

After everyone has been greeted well and engaged in a relaxed conversation, the group will come together. As mentioned earlier, set up the chairs in such a way that everyone can see everyone else's eyes and so that no one is in a perceived seat of prominence. This will create a "we're all equal when we are together" mindset. A sense of equality is vital if everyone is going to engage in the conversation and no one is given the right to dominate the conversation.

A tribal small-group experience has three phases: (1) Our Story, (2) His Story, and (3) The Journey. After spending significant time in the gospels, I found that in almost every transformational conversation Jesus was engaged in and no matter whom He was talking with, this was the actual flow of the conversation.

Our Story

The conversation will begin with Our Story, the story of the individuals in the group. For decades, a small-group Bible study began with the reading of Scripture. Obviously, God's story found in the Bible is ultimately the focal point of the experience and the primary way that God speaks to those in the group. But creating a longing to know what God is telling each group member and the group will make the experience more exciting than ever and will cause people to engage in the conversation with an intensity not often experienced. Getting a "forward lean" from group members is the key to a leader's being heard, group members' wanting to know what God is telling them, and engaging people intently in the conversation.

All great communicators know what the forward lean is. When an audience is in "forward lean" mode, they are tilting slightly forward on the edge of their seats waiting to hear what's next. The communicator has created a tension that must be relieved, and it will be relieved only when whatever question that's on the table has been answered or the issue at hand is resolved. People are most apt to be in the forward-lean position when a topic is first tied to their own life situation or their believed philosophy. Bottom line—people most want to hear what God has to say when His response is directly related to a life situation they have dealt with, are dealing with, or know they will be forced to deal with in the future. The forward lean is also created when there is tension between what someone believes and the most prevalent ideology in the group. Maybe this is why Jesus, in almost every instance, started with someone else's story before getting into His own.

In the gospels, Our Story can be seen in a personal need being revealed (the many times someone longed to be healed, a sick family member needed healing, someone had died, or an individual, like Zacchaeus, longed for his story to be redeemed), a question that someone needed answered (for example, the disciples asking Jesus what a parable meant), a past mistake that was haunting someone (for example, Peter after denying Jesus), or an ideological trap set by the cynical (for example, the Pharisees trying to trap Jesus).

Through a series of carefully crafted questions, experiences, and through other creative means, a tribal CMC leader must drive group members into forward-lean mode so that His Story can invade their own.

His Story

His Story comes in the form of God unearthing His truth and character through Scripture. It is a teaching, a declaration, a command, a sacrifice made, or a miraculous act revealed in the Bible done by or taught by God and discussed by the group. It is God's response to Our Story, often seen through Jesus, to someone's curiosity, someone's need, His knowledge of a crowd's needs, or a cynicism directed at Him. And when His Story responds with and intermingles with each group member's story, transformation is possible.

This part of the experience is especially intriguing with a true tribal small group because it includes some who are not yet convinced Christ is the only way to God or that He is God. The conversation must be led by someone who patiently allows the Bible to speak for itself without attacking or abrasively questioning those who are not yet followers of Christ. The group leader must remember that these individuals have courageously committed to the group to experiment with and/ or explore Christianity with a group of mostly Christ followers. They have joined for relationship. To push them to faith too quickly may be the end of the relationship and the end of their spiritual journey.

The pace of each explorer's journey is not determined by the small-group leader, it is determined by God. It will take some explorers weeks to understand and consider the faith, others months, and some years. A tribal CMC leader must allow the cynic to be cynical as long as necessary, the doubter to doubt for the time right for him, and the skeptic to slowly release his skepticism, which will create a hovering pessimism when the group gathers.

But as God's story integrates more fully with each group member's story, the journey toward full devotion will become more and more possible.

The Journey

The Journey section of the meeting encompasses three experiences: (1) a response to God's story, (2) how the group can be missional together, and (3) how the group can meet one another's needs.

1. A response to God's story—Once God's profound acts are revealed and discussed, a profound response is intuitive. In biblical times as well as today, no one can see God's astounding acts and attitude and not be moved to consider his or her own journey. After hearing what God has done and is willing to do, each group member must grapple with the next step. For some, that will be simply considering whether they can accept these antique stories as true and real. Someone else may be considering whether to make a great sacrifice, reveal a past or present sin, ask someone's forgiveness, or make major changes in some aspect of life. Other group members may be asking themselves if they can step across the line of faith and give the rest of their lives to Christ. The list could go on and on.

2. How the group will be missional together—This aspect of group life will be overlooked by many group leaders who have led groups in decades past. Being missional was then a secondary consideration, one that came to the forefront only if the church asked for help with something or there was a special event planned by the church staff. In this era, mission needs to be a group's primary responsibility because Christ was always missional and the group is to embody Christ. Also, those who are not yet followers of Christ are intuitively drawn to make a difference in the world. As these individuals are missional with the group, barriers will come down, those in the group who are Christ followers will be viewed as Christlike, and opportunities to speak of Christ will be made possible. Not only that, it's the right thing to do.

3. How the group can meet one another's needs — During this part of the gathering group members can pray for one another or let members know of a personal need that the group can meet.

The Journey section of the experience must be carefully orchestrated, allowing anyone to know he is always an equal part of the group no matter where he is in his journey. The atheist who proclaims that the biblical accounts are bunk and snickers when the group prays must leave the gathering as vividly aware that he is still as much a part of the group as the person who falls to his knees weeping before his Lord because he has committed a sin that seems insignificant to most of the people in the room. Every group member is journeying equally with each person at a different place on the path.

This three-stage experience will make it possible for every group member to know he or she is valued, make Christ the centerpiece of each gathering, and connect with anyone in the group no matter how far from or close to God he or she is at the time.

LEADING A TRIBAL DISCUSSION

Due to the makeup of a tribal CMC, the discussion's facilitator must be willing to reconsider a few aspects of the role:

Host a conversation rather than oversee a discussion.
In the past, a small-group leader often found himself asking one question after another. After various people in the group responded to a question, the leader then moved to the next question and the group members responded. That is, the leader oversaw a discussion. He owned and had control over each step of the discussion, and it flowed as he determined it would. In a tribal CMC, instead of overseeing a discussion, the facilitator must host a conversation. That is, the goal is for the entire group to engage with each other in such a way that questions asked by the group leader lead to the group members asking and responding to one another's questions. Each person becomes a secondary facilitator at some level. What we're trying to accomplish is something as relaxed as a conversation around a dinner table. If a group of friends gathered to have a meal together, one person wouldn't reign over the conversation. Someone might ask a question that guides the group in a direction. But someone else might move the conversation in a slightly different direction, and others around the table would respond. This is the normal and natural way that people converse with one another. Everyone is important to the conversation, and anyone can move the conversation in a slightly different direction without upending the conversation completely.

Let's say a tribal small group is meeting together and is discussing Jesus' healing of the paralytic in Mark 2. You'll recall this historic event. Four men lowered a paralyzed man through the roof of a house so that the man had a chance to be healed by Jesus. At first, instead of healing the man, Jesus simply said, "Son, your sins are forgiven" (verse 5). After some leading cynics question Jesus because they believe only God can forgive sins and they do not believe that Jesus is God, Jesus does heal the man.

There are several themes in this story: (1) friendship, (2) the level of sacrifice to be made for those who are impaired, (3) miracles, (4) Jesus as God, and the list could continue.

According to the makeup of the group that's gathered, this conversation could go in many directions. While the group leader needs to keep the group focused on the gospel as revealed in the story, it would be okay for the conversation to head down a path opened by a group member's curiosity. Maybe the least talkative person chimes in and brazenly asks, "How many of you really believe that Jesus did stuff like this?" It is vital that the group leader allow the conversation to head down this path. After the group responds affirmatively, establishing that Jesus has done and does do the miraculous, a logical next question might be: "So, if I push God hard enough He'll work the miracle I need?"

Ultimately the goal is to have a natural conversation based on the needs of the group continually focused on Scripture and the God of Scripture. As long as a group doesn't veer far from the primary theme of the Scripture passage being discussed, the natural flow of the conversation will resonate with group members much more than what seems to be a contrived experience that keeps group members from finding out what they are specifically longing to know.

Teach only when necessary. In a tribal CMC, revelation of God's truth is unearthed in conversation. A group leader must come to the group meeting (1) having asked the Holy Spirit to be the teacher, (2) prepared with a series of questions that will start and promote the conversation, and (3) fully aware of what the Bible is saying. A friend of mine once reminded me that a conversational Bible study can be "a night of shared ignorance." I have never forgotten that statement. It is a fact. An effective small-group leader is vividly aware that he or she is responsible for keeping any false truths from taking root while making it possible for truth to be unearthed through discussion. This is done by using a well-crafted series of questions, allowing the Holy Spirit to take the conversation in directions the leader hadn't anticipated, and redirecting the group back to the theme and truth of the passage when necessary. The small-group leader will need to take the reins of the conversation and guide it in the direction of truth if and when what is not God's truth is about to land and take root. Teach only when you must but teach if you must.

Remember that you may have three kinds of cynics in the room: (1) silent, (2) subtle, and (3) self-aware. *Silent cynics* seldom speak, and if they do, they don't unveil their cynicism. They don't want to rock the ideological boat, so if they do speak, they say what they believe the group wants to hear. *Subtle cynics* are very appropriate in their cynicism and may couch their cynicism in phrases like, "Some people believe . . ." or "I hear that most people think . . ." These individuals want to make a point without upending the group's core values. *Self-aware cynics* blatantly and unapologetically verbalize their disbelief and doubts.

Group leaders must know that each of these persons is likely present and will affect the gathering. Silent cynics will most likely discuss what they really think away from the group gathering. This passive-aggressive behavior affects only those who the silent cynic is speaking with and may or may not affect the person or group negatively. Subtle cynics create moments of frustration for group members. Because they are unwilling or unable to let the group know that they are talking about their own doubts, the group cannot face the cynics' beliefs head-on and journey with them in ways that would be transforming. *Self-aware cynics* are a gift to a small group. These individuals force group members to conclude whether they have embraced the ideals of their parents or other people they have respected rather than establishing a faith of their own. While the self-aware cynic may bring the facilitator some cringe factor, he or she will say things that let mature believers respond with what silent and subtle cynics need to hear to move beyond their cynicism.

Allow the group time to process the meaning of a passage together rather than telling the group the meaning of the passage. Because many today believe that everyone makes his or her own truth, we want to be sure we're using the most effective way to ascertain truth. A community in agreement carries more weight than a lone facilitator declaring what is right. In fact, if a facilitator declares what the truth is and seems to expect everyone else to simply agree, it may seem like just another opinion rather than the biblical bottom line. Be certain of this though: If a group is embracing falsity, the leader must redirect group members toward truth and guide them to process what is right together. In most cases the Holy Spirit will be at work, and the group will likely land on truth rather than accept an outrageous opinion birthed in ignorance.

When you're leading the discussion, remember that you are discussing the Great Narrative. A few things you'll want to consider:

1. *Remind your group that the Bible is the Story told through many stories.* It is the story of redemption unveiled through many situations.
2. *Put God's expectations or dos and don'ts in context.* Every announcement of dos and don'ts takes place in the context of an individual or a community's story. Guide your group to discuss these rights and wrongs in light of the context in which that story is being told. But be sure

group members don't conclude they are not held to the same standards as those in the story.

3. ***Guide your group to discuss who God is in light of His actions and activities.*** Every story reveals something about God, a personality trait or an attribute of His character. Some of the most life-transforming conversations a group has take place when the group discusses who God is in light of how He performed in a real-life situation. I assure you that group members will see a much bigger God than they currently perceive Him to be when discussing the complexities of His character, actions, and decisions. This will stretch them, but it will give them a more realistic view of Him.

4. ***Let each character in the story come to life.*** When discussing the story's characters, interpret their statements and actions in light of who they were, who they represented, the role they played in the society they were in, and the culture in which they lived.

5. ***Guide each member to conclude which character in the story most intersects with his or her own.*** In most cases each group member sees something of himself or herself in one of the story's characters. Help group members conclude why they do. It is very possible that some unstated pain or loss or reason for celebrating God's power in the past will become known for the first time.

AN AWKWARD TENSION

Let's be honest: Group leaders may experience an awkward tension among CMC members who have differing viewpoints,

especially when those viewpoints flow from varying worldviews.
This tension may never be eliminated, but it can be diminished.
A few things you should keep in mind:

- People are used to being with people who are polar
  opposites on many issues. This is the makeup of the
  world in which we live. The tension a leader feels may be
  self-imposed.
- Most people are able and willing to share opposing
  views as long as they sense that they are still respected by
  the leader and the other group members. Show honor
  to anyone in the group who shares openly, even if the
  opinion he or she shares is incorrect. But be careful:
  Honor them for speaking openly without affirming their
  incorrect interpretation of God's words. Also, thank
  members for respecting those whose views differ from
  their own. But thank them for showing respect, not for
  agreeing with that which contradicts Scripture.
- Don't lecture group members or let group members
  lecture one another. There is nearly nothing as demean-
  ing as someone in the group going on a rant, especially
  when that rant is aimed at another member. Ultimately,
  both the person being lectured and the person giving the
  lecture will feel guilty for elevating the level of tension in
  the room.
- Create an environment that welcomes honesty and
  authenticity. In a tribal CMC, honesty and authenticity
  are keys that open the door to a relaxed atmosphere. Until
  a group agrees that the words of God trump all others,
  which could take months or years, agreeing that all will be
  honest and authentic without anyone casting judgment

on others for doing so will lower the level of tension immediately. It may be important to include this in the group agreement and remind group members of this agreement often.

In a tribal CMC, the group doesn't change what it discusses. It simply discusses it differently. Dogmatism is set aside for diplomatic discussion. Lectures are replaced by communal understandings unearthed in conversation through the power of the Holy Spirit. Debates over what is truth are replaced with respectful deliberation seeking truth. And when the group includes those on a journey toward Christ but still struggling with the Bible and Christianity, tolerance is replaced with acceptance of the people without finding it necessary to argue them into ideological submission.

THE GOSPEL

The gospel is more relevant than ever. It is the story of Jesus from before time began and is a never-ending story. It is the revelation of the Son of God coming, dying, rising from the dead, and returning to take His children home. It is the story that will resonate with even the most cynical of all tribal group members. It must be told now more than ever because:

We are a generation of story. Storytelling is no longer an art form for professionals; it is a routine woven into the fabric of everyday existence and used by us everydayers. When we get together, we describe in great detail the standout experience of the day, we tell the story depicted in the latest film we saw or book we read, we tell stories of our childhood, and we sometimes try to repeat the story used as illustration in the last sermon we heard. We may not remember the sermon topic, but the story sticks. Storytelling is as intuitive today as debating politics was in previous generations.

Even the media has picked up on this. When major sporting events are soon to be broadcast, the players' lives are beautifully and emotionally recounted. We are taken to the ghetto to see their childhood homes, meet their friends, and see interviews of family members. We not only long to know their stats, we long to know their stories.

Storytelling demands nonbelievers wrestle with the gospel. In a time when "truth" is often perceived by those outside the faith as nonexistent, story may be the most potent and powerful witnessing tool. When we tell our stories of how Jesus' story transformed ours, the person we're talking to is forced to reckon with the power of Jesus' story, which is the gospel.

The family is disintegrating. The gospel is the story of a perfect Father and His relationship with His Son. In an era when 50 percent or more of households with children no longer include both of the children's birth parents, the story of Jesus and His relationship with Father God resonates with those whose hearts long for family wholeness. This is especially true of men whose fathers abandoned the family.

Society is void of heroes. In an era when narcissism rules the day, heroes seem nonexistent. Culture seems to scream, "Look out for and protect yourself above all others!" Heroes do just the opposite. They sacrifice themselves for others. The human heart longs for and is moved by stories of heroes. The gospel is the story of the greatest of all heroes, Jesus Christ. He left utopia to be brutally murdered in order to save the eternal lives of every person who acknowledged the truth of His story and embraced its power.

The gospel is the story of stories, the only story that can turn a cynic into a fanatic; a spiritually abused church hater into a lover of Jesus' bride, the church; a Buddhist into a person clinging to the one true God. The gospel is the hope of the world and eternal life to every individual who ever walks through the front door of any home to attend a group gathering.

CMC leaders must believe it, love it, tell it, and live it. When they do, those far from Christ will see and consider Jesus.

BETWEEN GATHERINGS

What happens between gatherings is more vital than ever. Why?

Friends hang out together. Let's say it again: Relationships in a tribal CMC must be natural and authentic. If people are friends, they get together not because there's a scheduled meeting but just because they like being together. If a group gets together only when there's a scheduled gathering, some in the group won't believe that the people in the group are in relationship. Rather, they'll believe they are expected to attend a required weekly experience. This one thing will keep the group from experiencing transformed lives, and in most cases, those who are not yet followers of Christ will bail.

The most effective transformational conversations often take place between gatherings. The group gathering will start a conversation, but it will only be the start if a group leader is wise. You see, during a group gathering, a group leader seldom gets unbridled opinion from every group member. In fact, no matter how often we speak of the freedom to talk openly and the responsibility to keep all that takes place in the meeting confidential, many will still hold their ideological cards close to the chest. If a group leader wants to know what is really going on, he will need to spend time with members between gatherings. This doesn't have to be a one-on-one conversation, although it may be necessary sometimes. If some of the group members get together to have coffee or share a meal together, if the topic from the last meeting is brought up, oftentimes the silent group member will speak out. He has probably been wishing he would have spoken at the meeting and isn't going to miss the opportunity again.

Pray for every group member by name daily. Prayer is the number one reason people are transformed. In their book *Small Groups, Big Impact*, Jim Egli and Dwight Marable said,

> Our research, involving thousands of small groups, dramatically underlines the simple biblical truth: When we pray, we see God do awesome things! If you want others drawn to Jesus and their lives changed, pray. If you want Jesus' life flowing to you and through you, draw near to him. Life-giving ministry depends on God and his abilities not on you and your abilities.[1]

They continued,

> Our research reveals that leaders with a strong prayer life have groups that are more than four times more fruitful evangelistically. Of the leaders with a strong prayer life, 83% reported that their group had seen someone come to Christ in the past 9 months, but only 19% of the leaders with a weak prayer life could say the same.[2]

Please don't miss this. The most important thing a small-group leader does is pray for those he is leading. The wisest of small-group leaders realizes and accepts that he is not the one who prompts someone to start a relationship with Jesus; the Holy Spirit is. He also understands he is not the one who transforms the hearts of those who are believers. The leader works in tandem with the Holy Spirit in the process but ultimately the leader's responsibility is to create an environment where the work of God can take place. Prayer between gatherings is the key.

CHAPTER 9

CHRISTIAN MICRO-COMMUNITIES THAT REALLY MATTER

G roups that make the greatest impact see beyond themselves and realize they can influence more people with the gospel as well as generations to come if they are strategically and purposefully involved in being unapologetically and powerfully evangelistic and by birthing new groups. But this will need to look different than it has in the past.

EVANGELISM

Evangelism will always have as its goal to make the gospel known and allow it to do its work. This will be unchanging throughout all of human history. And each generation must consider the era and spiritual climate in which it's been planted and respond accordingly. A few movements illustrate this well.

During what many call the Billy Graham era, large gatherings were effective beyond imagination. It seemed that whether Graham was preaching at a stadium event or a guest preacher was preaching a series of services at a rural Kentucky church, individuals who were not yet followers of Christ would show up, walk down an aisle, and start an eternal friendship with Jesus.

Most would laugh out loud at such an idea today. Unbelievers won't come and believers won't bring them. In most cases, this model isn't effective today. This shouldn't surprise us. Let's not forget that during the Billy Graham era, most people in the West were fully aware that Jesus was the Son of God and that, in order to be connected to God, one must accept Christ as Savior and Lord. The concepts necessary for a transforming experience were already in the average person; those who were not yet followers of Christ simply needed a time and place to step across the line of faith and begin their Christian journey.

Before too long, we became aware that people were no longer drawn to large evangelistic services. The Billy Graham era had passed. People would still attend church and most even held it in high regard, but the experience needed to connect with pre-Christians where they were. Thus, the seeker movement was born. During this era, followers of Christ were encouraged to invite their unbelieving friends to attend a "seeker service." Believers were promised an experience that would not embarrass the unchurched; the "talks" would relate to real life. The arts were a big part of this movement. Dramatic presentations were used often. A dramatic sketch would take the audience to a point of high tension, then leave them hanging, without bringing resolve to oftentimes very intense, real-life situations. It could be a teenager at odds with a parent or a husband and wife on the verge of divorce. The teaching pastor would then use God's words found in the Bible to teach what God would have people do in these situations and how He would be at work in each of these circumstances.

Over time and after attending many services, experiences carefully crafted for the comfort of those seeking to know about Christianity, a person would consider crossing the line of faith.

This movement made sense in a world where the church still had substantial credibility. Most had attended church as a child but the old way of doing church seemed antiquated and boring, so coming to church to hear a kickin' band and a relevant sermon was exciting. Most still believed God's Word was advantageous to understanding and knowing how to respond to life's many difficult and confusing circumstances, so coming to a church to learn God's solutions to difficult life issues made sense.

But God didn't place us in the Billy Graham or the seeker-sensitive era. Most of those far from Christ today will never show up for a revival service or a citywide crusade, and most will be reluctant to attend a weekend worship experience, even if the senior pastor is offering answers to life's most difficult questions. Let's face it—anyone can find a communicator answering life's questions on YouTube, and the answer will be given in five minutes, not forty-five.

If we are going to see pre-Christians become Christians, we have to rethink evangelism. We've entered a new era, one that demands the right response. Doug Schaupp said it well when he wrote about the necessary shift as he was doing evangelism on a college campus:

> When the campus first entered the twilight zone of post-modernity, we knew we were in for a ride. In the early 1990's we could feel the tectonic plates shifting underneath us on campus. The students we worked with increasingly viewed the world around them in entirely different ways from what we were accustomed to. Though the tremors of change had been around for decades, the big "postmodern" shift became unavoidable in the 1990's. Students weren't responding in the same ways they had before. Sharing the truth of Jesus' gospel no longer moved people.[1]

Doug and his cowriter, Don Everts, went on to tell us that there are five thresholds of postmodern conversion that take place in the life of a postmodern moving toward an acceptance of the gospel:

- From distrust to trust
- From complacent to curious
- From being closed to change to being open to change in his or her life
- From meandering to seeking
- Crossing the threshold of the kingdom itself [2]

Obviously, not every person's pathway into an authentic, game-changing connection with Christ is the same.

Remember this: For most people living in today's world, becoming a follower of Christ is a journey, not an event. And this journey is done best in a healthy CMC.

Every group leader needs to recognize that in many instances, the road to faith in Christ is long and will demand a willingness to patiently walk alongside pre-Christians in his or her CMC. Every group leader needs to know that creating a safe environment where pre-Christians can voice their differences of opinion without being judged is a necessity. Every group leader needs to understand that the group he or she leads must be willing to accept that each of the group members is a fellow journeyer in a fallen world and that, while many of them may have already crossed the line to faith, the leader is responsible to help others join them there. And most of all, the group leader must help members realize that they will do this best by exhibiting the love of Christ for a long time instead of walking the unbeliever through a canned presentation as soon as possible.

There is no better place than a tribal CMC for a not-yet follower of Christ in today's world to experience Christian community and go on a journey toward faith. It is the perfect place to ask questions, wrestle with flawed understandings, see the love of Christ through the actions of others, experience faith at work, and see and hear the gospel at work.

MULTIPLICATION

If there were a biblical small group within walking distance of every person on the planet, the world would experience the power of the gospel. This can happen if and only if small groups are willing to multiply.

The multiplication of a CMC simply means that like an amoeba that splits, one group becomes two. The DNA remains the same in both life forms, but there are two of them now.

In small-group world past, multiplication of a group started with a leader choosing an apprentice for a preexisting or new group. One of the leader's responsibilities was to mentor the apprentice, knowing that the apprentice would someday leave the present group, take part of the group with him, and start a group of his own. The present leader would continue to lead the part of the group that remained, find a new apprentice, and continue to start groups that start groups.

In years past, it was appropriate and right to multiply a group every eighteen to twenty-four months. Statistics had proved that a group that didn't multiply within two years would most likely never multiply, and because multiplication of a group is the means through which more people can be involved in a life-transforming group, this speed of multiplication was very important.

As we consider tribal CMCs, we find ourselves with a

complex dilemma: How do we multiply a group this often and still have group members experience the life transformation that we long for them to know? A group multiplying every eighteen months, even every two years, will be hard-pressed to see the levels of transformation it deserves. For various reasons, it may take eighteen months to two years for a leader to be perceived as trustworthy enough to gain any level of influence. Not only that, it may take two years for an individual to embrace God's Word as real and authentic. It may take two years for a not-yet follower of Christ to start believing that the Christians in the group are accepting him out of love instead of obligation. To multiply a group before these things are established will be spiritually traumatic and throw the brakes on what God longs to do in individual lives. Also, the multiplication of a group is an easy exit ramp out of group life. A core of the group may need to consider being together for a very long haul, and everyone in the group needs to know he or she will be doing group life with the same people for a long time.

Here are three creative ways for growth a CMC might consider, options that will allow a group to multiply while keeping a high level of relational consistency:

1. ***Groups of six.*** Six people remain together for a long time or lifetime while continuing to welcome a new group of six to join them every eighteen to twenty-four months. One of the persons in the new group of six is the apprentice of the established group leader. When . the time to multiply comes, the original group of six continues their journey together as does the six that joined their group. Each group of six connects with another group of six, an apprentice is chosen, and in

eighteen to twenty-four months the process is repeated. Using this idea, a group of six will continue their journey together for many years while being on mission to regularly start a new group.

2. *Geographically based groups training new leaders.* Many churches are already using geographically based groups. That is, groups gathering together based on the proximity of the meeting location. Obviously, these groups don't multiply in usual ways. But they can be on mission to start new groups. Every eighteen to twenty-four months a geographically based group can take on an apprentice or two, future leaders located in an untouched area of the city. After the apprentices have concluded their training, they then start a new group in their own community. Each group continues to do this, and before long, the entire community has a biblically functioning CMC within walking distance of every home. In this situation, neighbors continue to do group together while at the same time they are helping to establish new groups on streets and cul-de-sacs around the city.

3. *Lifetime groups that send out leaders.* Great small-group leaders will be constantly evaluating group members they are leading to see which of them has leadership potential. When they find someone, they ask him if he would be willing to make a great sacrifice for the kingdom and, when he is ready, go lead a group of his own. This is the principle that drives this concept. A group may remain together for a lifetime and still send someone off every two years to start a group of his own. This demands that a small-group leader have the starting of new groups as a high priority and that the leader consistently reminds

members that they are praying for and in the process of seeing who in the group will leave to start a new mission elsewhere. This type of group multiplication is most difficult as most of the group remains together and one must make a major sacrifice. But if the small-group leader constantly keeps that vision in front of the group, some will perceive it a great honor to be asked to start a group of their own.

Concerning multiplication and language in the new tribal CMC era: For many years the small-group community has used phrases like "split the group," "multiply the group," or "birth a new group." While each of these phrases is very descriptive, they each still reek of a painful experience demanded by the church leadership. I suggest using "starting a new mission" when talking about multiplying a small group. We live in a missionally minded world made up of a people who long to be on mission, meeting the needs of others and caring for those less fortunate. This terminology will reinforce the importance of being the mission house for the street, cul-de-sac, or subdivision where the group is meeting, a motivation that is real and that resonates positively with group members.

OPEN OR CLOSED GROUPS?

Many of us have embraced a fallacy, a fallacy that has been hindering evangelism through our groups. We've been telling our leaders that closed small groups are the only road to deeper intimacy among members, and because one of the primary goals of a group is personal openness (sharing) and vulnerability, the group can and should be closed. It makes logical sense. It makes sense when considering group dynamics. But it just isn't true, and a tribal CMC will embrace this fact.

Jim Egli and Dwight Marable wrote,

> We were curious to see if open groups that are actively seeking and including new people could, in fact, experience the same level of loving relationships as closed groups. We were startled by what the statistical analysis showed. Open groups actually experience significantly more community than closed groups![3]

A few paragraphs later:

> The results are so strong that we can actually tell you that if you want to experience deeper community in your small group, you should make it an open group that is actively reaching out to others! And, on the other hand, if you want a superficial level of relationships within the group and between its members, it would be best to make it a closed group.[4]

We can now with integrity tell our group leaders that their groups will be relationally closer by consistently welcoming guests to the gatherings. Groups will be able to simultaneously accomplish the ultimate goal and command: "Go therefore and make disciples of all nations, baptizing them in the name of the Father and of the Son and of the Holy Spirit, teaching them to observe all that I have commanded you. And behold, I am with you always, to the end of the age" (Matthew 28:19-20).

Even in a tribal CMC, it's important to reach out to people who are far from a connection to Christ and welcome them into your CMC—anytime.

A FINAL WORD FROM THE AUTHOR

I have one dream: to see a biblical small group within walking distance of every person on the planet. I believe with every ounce of my being that in today's world the most effective way to "go therefore and make disciples of all nations, baptizing them in the name of the Father and of the Son and of the Holy Spirit, teaching them to observe all that I have commanded you" (Matthew 28:19-20) is through biblical CMCs that are open to outsiders, welcoming the power of the Holy Spirit, and willing to make the gospel the primary component of their conversations. I am praying for an army of like-minded small-group types to join me in this calling. If you are one of those people, I'd love to hear from you. E-mail me at rick.howerton@navpress.com.

About five times a week, I share information for small-group leaders, small-group pastors and coaches, and church leaders on my blog. If you'd like to subscribe or just check in once in a while, go to http://blogs.navpress.com/rickhowerton/My-Blog. I also try to encourage ministry groups through tweets via Twitter. If you'd like to be a Twitter follower, my Twitter title is @rickhowerton.

Most of all, I hope you'll join me as we plant a biblical small group within walking distance of every person on planet Earth.

NOTES

CHAPTER 1: FACING A NEW REALITY

1. See an image of the print "Saying Grace" at http://www.flickr.com/photos/x-ray_delta_one/3943961665.

CHAPTER 2: A DELICATE NOSEDIVE INTO THE NEW REALITY

1. Kenneth Boa and Gail Burnett, *Pursuing Wisdom* (Colorado Springs, CO: NavPress, 1999), 26.
2. Belinda Luscombe, "Are Marriage Statistics Divorced from Reality?" *Time*, May 24, 2010, http://www.time.com/time/magazine/article/0,9171,1989124,00.html.
3. Ed Stetzer, Richie Stanley, and Jason Hayes, *Lost and Found: The Younger Unchurched and the Churches That Reach Them* (Nashville: B&H Publishing, 2009), 81.
4. Julia Duin, *Quitting Church* (Grand Rapids, MI: Baker, 2008), 121.
5. Andy Braner, *An Exposé on Teen Sex and Dating* (Colorado Springs, CO: NavPress, 2011), 26.
6. Braner, 108.

CHAPTER 4: CREATING HEALTHY TRIBAL CHRISTIAN MICRO-COMMUNITIES

1. David Kinnaman, *Unchristian* (Grand Rapids, MI: Baker, 2007), 11.
2. Kinnaman, 27.
3. Jim Egli and Dwight Marable, *Small Groups, Big Impact* (Saint Charles, IL: ChurchSmart Resources, 2011), 12.
4. Egli and Marable, 79.

5. Dan B. Allender, *To Be Told* (Colorado Springs, CO: WaterBrook Press, 2005), 14.

6. Calvin Miller, *Miracles and Wonders* (Brentwood, TN: Warner Faith, 2003), 21.

7. Wayne Grudem, *Systematic Theology* (Grand Rapids, MI: Zondervan, 1994), 359.

8. Grudem, 360.

9. Julia Duin, *Quitting Church* (Grand Rapids, MI: Baker, 2008), 33.

10. For more on this topic, see Roc Bottomly, *The Promised Power: Experiencing the Union of Word and Spirit* (Colorado Springs, CO: NavPress, 2005).

11. George Barna, *Growing True Disciples* (Ventura, CA: Issachar Resources, 2000), 19.

12. Barna, 77–78.

13. Mark Kelly, "LifeWay Research Finds Parents Churches Can Help Teens Stay in Church," LifeWay, August 7, 2007, http://www .lifeway.com/ArticleView?storeId=10054&catalogId=10001& langId=-1&article=LifeWay-Research-finds-parents-churches -can-help-teens-stay-in-church, accessed December 5, 2011.

14. Ed Stetzer, Richie Stanley, and Jason Hayes, *Lost and Found* (Nashville: B&H Publishing, 2009), 83.

15. Stetzer, Stanley, and Hayes, 125–127.

16. Randall Neighbour, *The Naked Truth About Small Group Ministry* (Houston: Touch Publications, 2009), 203.

17. Neighbour, 203.

CHAPTER 5: THE FOUR QUADRANTS OF GROUP LIFE

1. Wayne Grudem, *Systematic Theology* (Grand Rapids, MI: Zondervan, 1994), 1255.

2. "Barna Survey Examines Changes in Worldview Among Christians over the Past 13 Years," The Barna Group, March 6, 2009, http://www.barna.org/barna-update/article/21 -transformation/252-barna-survey-examines-changes-in -worldview-among-christians-over-the-past-13-years, accessed January 3, 2012.

3. Joseph H. Hellerman, *When the Church Was a Family: Recapturing Jesus' Vision for Authentic Christian Community* (Nashville: B&H Academic, 2009), 36.

4. John Burke, *No Perfect People Allowed* (Grand Rapids, MI: Zondervan, 2005), 288–289.

5. M. Scott Boren, *Missional Small Groups* (Grand Rapids, MI: Baker, 2010), 34.

CHAPTER 6: THE MAKEUP OF A TRIBAL SMALL GROUP

1. Seth Godin, *Tribes* (New York: Portfolio, 2008), 1–2.

2. T. W. Hunt, *Seeing the Unseen* (Colorado Springs, CO: NavPress, 2011), 14.

3. Wayne Grudem, *Systematic Theology* (Grand Rapids, MI: Zondervan, 1994), 627.

CHAPTER 8: THE TRIBAL CHRISTIAN MICRO-COMMUNITY GATHERING

1. Jim Egli and Dwight Marable, *Small Groups, Big Impact* (Saint Charles, IL: ChurchSmart Resources, 2011), 25.

2. Egli and Marable, 24–25.

CHAPTER 9: CHRISTIAN MICRO-COMMUNITIES THAT REALLY MATTER

1. Don Everts and Doug Schaupp, *I Once Was Lost* (Downers Grove, IL: InterVarsity, 2008), 12–13.

2. Everts and Schaupp, 23–24.

3. Jim Egli and Dwight Marable, *Small Groups, Big Impact* (Saint Charles, IL: ChurchSmart Resources, 2011), 37.

4. Egli and Marable, 37.

ABOUT THE AUTHOR

RICK HOWERTON has one passion: to see "a biblical small group within walking distance of every person on the planet." He is currently pursuing this passion as the national small-group strategist for NavPress, spearheading its small-group publishing efforts. Rick has authored or coauthored several books, studies, and leader training resources, including *Destination Community: Small-Group Ministry Manual*, *The Gospel and the Truth: Living the Message of Jesus*, *Small Group Life Ministry Manual: A New Approach to Small Groups*, *Redeeming the Tears: A Journey Through Grief and Loss*, *Small Group Life: Kingdom*, *Small-Group Kickoff Retreat: Experiential Training for Group Leaders*, and *Great Beginnings: Your First Small-Group Study*. Rick's varied ministry experiences as a collegiate minister, small-group pastor, teaching pastor, elder, full-time trainer, church consultant, and successful church planter give him a perspective of church life that is all-encompassing and multidimensional. Rick is highly sought after for speaking and training.

More from NavPress
for small-group leaders

Connecting in Communities
Eddie Mosley

This practical guide takes pastors and leaders from conception to implementation of a small-group ministry.

978-1-61521-685-7

101 Ways to Reach Your Community
Steve Sjogren

You and your church can share God's love with others through these practical, valuable, easy-to-implement ideas.

978-1-57683-220-2

101 Ways to Help People in Need
Steve and Janie Sjogren

Your community is filled with people in need. Use these simple and creative ways to reach out to them.

978-1-57683-315-5

To order copies, call NavPress at **1-800-366-7788** or log on to **www.NavPress.com**.

NAVPRESS
Discipleship Inside Out®

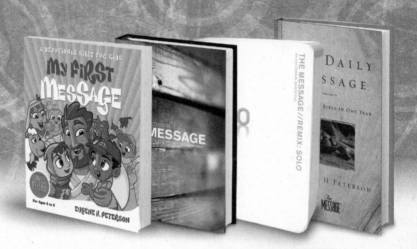

N A V E S S E N T I A L S

Voices of The Navigators—Past, Present, and Future

NavEssentials offer core Navigator messages from such authors as Jim Downing, LeRoy Eims, Mike Treneer, and more — at an affordable price. This new series will deeply influence generations in the movement of discipleship. Learn from the old and new messages of The Navigators how powerful and transformational the life of a disciple truly is.

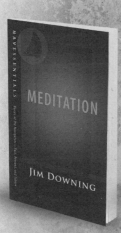

Meditation
by Jim Downing
9781615217250 | $5.00

Advancing the Gospel
by Mike Treneer
9781617471575 | $5.00

Laboring in the Harvest
by LeRoy Eims with Randy Eims
9781615216406 | $10.99

To order, go to **www.NavPress.com** or call **1-800-366-7788**.

NAVPRESS
Discipleship Inside Out®

SUPPORT THE MINISTRY OF THE NAVIGATORS

The Navigators' calling is to advance the gospel of Jesus and His kingdom into the nations through spiritual generations of laborers living and discipling among the lost.

Navigators have invested their lives in people for more than 75 years, coming alongside them life on life to help them passionately know Christ and to make Him known.

The U.S. Navigators' ministry touches lives in varied settings, including college campuses, military bases, downtown offices, urban neighborhoods, prisons, and youth camps.

Dedicated to helping people navigate spiritually, The Navigators aims to make a permanent difference in the lives of people around the world. The Navigators helps its communities of friends to follow Christ passionately and equip them effectively to go out and do the same.

To learn more about donating to The Navigators' ministry,
go to **www.navigators.org/us/support**
or call toll-free at **1-866-568-7827**.